Dear Larry 10/2011

The Chronicles of Moses

The Acts of an Apostolic Journey

You a true Yokefellow

Moses Vegh

With Ernest Weaver

Shalom

Moses

949-632-5060

The Chronicles of Moses
The Acts of an Apostolic Journey

Moses Vegh
Ambassadors of Hope to the Nations
P. O. Box 3337 San Clemente, CA 92673

moses@mosesvegh.org
www.mosesvegh.org

"Illustrations by David Beal
www.davidbealportraits.com"

© Moses Vegh 2013

ISBN 978-0-9895577-0-2

Weaver Publishing
9214 Madina Pkwy
Fort Wayne, Indiana 46825

Ernest Weaver
Phone (260) 750-0691
www.weaverpublishing.com

Acknowledgements

I am very grateful for the dedication and giftings of our editor and publisher Ernie Weaver. He has spent many hours editing my musings. Ernie has proven his skills and I highly recommend his expertise that can help many emerging writers, and even novices at writing like me.

We give thanks for all the many fine writers, scholars, exegetes and anointed prophetic voices that have spurred me on and have help motivate my "little raft" on my apostolic journey. I am indebted to my dear friend David Beal who is a design artist at Hallmark Cards. He masterfully illustrated my journey from the babe in the basket to my final destination. David also helped with the cover design. I also want to express a sincere thank you to the many fellow ministers who have influenced and blessed me over the years. I am eager to meet with you again in this book as we relive together the many exciting days we shared in one or more of the more than 80 countries to which we were commissioned as "Ambassadors of Hope."

Thanks always and in all things to my dear wife Betty who has been my faithful companion for over sixty years. She is mother to Debbie, Tom, Becky, Marcus (in Heaven), Cathy, and Michael, nineteen grandkids, and five great granddaughters. She has poured over every word of these manuscripts and has earned my respectful admiration as "Critique in Chief" as well as chief critic. Betty is my very best friend in the world.

Above all I want to express glory and honor and praise to Him who has washed us in His own blood and made us to be a kingdom of priests and kings unto our God.[1] Shalom!

---

[1] Revelation 1:5-6

Dedication

This book is dedicated to our beloved son,
Marcus, in whom we are well pleased.

Marcus Stephen Vegh
Born December 14, 1959.
Promoted to Heaven, October 20, 2007

About The Author

Two old vets: Moses and Pat Robertson

These *Chronicles of Moses* truly set forth the pathway of an apostolic journey. I have known Moses and his son Marcus (in whose memory this book is dedicated) for over 30 years. Father and son have served with me in the Freedom Council for several years. Moses has also ministered on several occasions to our CBN staff in prophetic conferences, and has been a guest on our 700 club at various times. This Chronicle contains unconventional time proven wisdom, which is very insightful, illuminating and impactful for this generation. This is a commentary on the faithfulness of God watching over His word to perform it! This is a "must read" which I am delighted to endorse.

Dr. Pat Robertson

Moses Vegh is a walking, talking, spiritual encyclopedia, ordained and anointed by God. I cherish the times God allows me to sit, learn and listen to a man who has deep and unique insight into God's word and will. The *Chronicles of Moses* is guaranteed to challenge all of us to grow into God's special purpose.

Doug Kelley

Founder: Open Arms Ministries, Los Angeles, California

The Chronicles of Moses

Moses Vegh has been a mentor and friend of mine for over three decades. He reminds me of Elisha, who purposefully forfeited all of his worldly opportunities to follow the Lord all the days of his life. I often say that Moses has gone where angels fear to tread. He's nearing eighty years of age and his voice and prophetic message is as strong today as it was when we first met thirty years ago through the Beal family in Detroit, Michigan.

We officially connected when he planned an Ohio delegation to attend the Washington for Jesus event. As our friendship with the entire Vegh family developed I came to realize and respect that no vision was too great for them to embrace. He is always encouraging others to "go for the things of God."

Because of the inspiration of Moses and partnering with other ministry friends like David Kitely and Paul Stern, we've travelled from China to Russia advancing the Kingdom of God. I've been on trains and planes with him throughout third world countries and he is always charged up ready for action. He's never met a stranger as a true evangelist for God. His prophetic gifting has challenged many others to go where they would not normally go, do what they would not normally do, and say what they might not normally say. He is an Ambassador for Christ. This book will certainly be an inspiration to discover what it's *really* like to forsake all *to follow Jesus.*

Daryl T. Sanders
Former Detroit Lions professional football player
Former senior pastor: Zion Church, Columbus, Ohio

Moses Vegh has an unquenchable passion and desire to see the Great Commission completed in this generation as you will soon read in his book *The Chronicles of Moses.* He has devoted his life to finishing the task commanded to us by our Lord and Savior Jesus Christ. Moses passed this longing and passion to his son, Marcus Vegh, who carried the torch and, in turn, passed it on to countless others who are carrying it today. I am one of those who were blessed by God to see this insatiable passion in both Moses and Marcus. I too am now carrying the torch, and I am eager to see how God will bless those that read this book, take the torch, and join the movement of finishing the task, until all have heard the wonderful redemptive message of Jesus Christ.

Hector Tamez Jr.
President ILAM

The Chronicles of Moses

"*Chronicles* is the uplifting and faith challenging account of the impact of one man - and his family - on the nations of the world. From his roots as a Hungarian immigrant, the blessing of God has rested on his ministry - from Cuba to Russia and beyond. You will be captivated by his faith, his commitment, and his determination to trust God in every circumstance of life."

Paul Eshleman
Vice-President, Campus Crusade for Christ

Too often the Lord's saints are promoted to heaven leaving nary a trace of their exploits for future generations. Gratefully, Moses Vegh hasn't let that happen. Though we've been friends for decades, reading Moses' book opened for me a whole new understanding of the intricate and amazing ways God has guided the Veghs' journey, one producing global impact and lasting fruit. You will find *The Chronicles of Moses* warm, engaging, and rich in transferable life lessons.

John D. Beckett
Author, *Loving Monday* and *Mastering Monday*
Chairman, The Beckett Companies, Elyria, Ohio

Even though *The Chronicles of Moses* is not a book of the Bible, it certainly reads like one. Moses Vegh has had more encounters with the Holy Spirit's miraculous moving than a hundred less adventurous souls. Just like his namesake, he has boldly taken a stand for righteousness in an ungodly culture, led multitudes out of bondage and seen countless signs and wonders throughout a long and storied life and ministry.

Meeting Moses Vegh also led to another great honor—having the privilege of knowing and working with his son, Marcus, who became an invaluable part of our team here at World Harvest Church. Marcus joined us at a critical time when we were building the largest church complex in three states and designing the infrastructure that would become one of the largest media ministries in the world. His tireless devotion to those tasks laid the groundwork for our future success. I could not be more pleased that this book is dedicated to him.

Pastor Rod Parsley
World Harvest Church, Columbus, Ohio

The Chronicles of Moses

Moses Vegh has been my pastor since the moment I was placed in his hands to be dedicated to the Lord as an infant. He has been a trusted mentor, advisor, counselor and co-laborer in the ministry of the gospel for the entirety of my life. There is no one more qualified to communicate the truths of *The Chronicles of Moses, the Acts of an Apostolic Journey."* His entire life and decades of ministry have been the truest example of an apostolic life and is a treasure in the church of our Lord Jesus around the world. You will be challenged by the wisdom, depth and passion of the revelation you are about to read and I am confident that it will transform your life. For this revelation has not come through the process of study alone but has been lived, and lived well, with fullness of joy. It is my great honor to highly recommend this book and this man.

> David Frech
> Lead Pastor
> Church of the Harvest
> Olathe, Kansas

I highly recommend "Chronicles of Moses" to any and every Christian who has ever thought of taking the Good News of Christ to people in other nations. For close to 40 years, Moses has made multiple trips to Hong Kong and many parts of China to preach, teach, prophesy and pour his heart into our people. I meet people in China all the time who remember his ministry, and many testify that ministry was the changing point of their lives. And the amazing thing is he is still going just as strong as ever! His testimony is both exciting and challenging, for we still have a great task before us as we labor to bring in this last-day harvest.

> Dennis Balcombe
> Revival Christian Church.

The Chronicles of Moses

Foreword

This book contains unconventional time proven wisdom, which is exceptionally insightful, illuminating, and impacting. Moses has cleverly woven together the lifelong chronicle of accumulated knowledge with his school of hard knocks experiences into a coherent package which is relatable to all generations.

This chronicle is not only an eye opener, but it will also elevate your faith level with a very balanced approach. His story is an honest assessment of successes and failures, hardships and heartbreaks, as well as unexpected victories and sovereign miracles.

Moses has been blessed to be closely associated with some of the so-called biggest and best in the Christian celebrity world and has still remained reachable and touchable as an instrument used of God to restore bruised and fallen comrades without breaking confidences.

Moses has more "best friends" than most people have socks, as this book will reveal. If you have spent fifteen minutes in his presence, you are a friend for life and will never be forgotten. He will always remember your name or your face, so you had better make a good impression the first time.

Even though he is now in his eighties he has never wished to acknowledge his age. This has kept him fresh, and flourishing, and unwilling to slow down his horrendous non-stop travel schedule. He has always had an uncanny ability to remain totally focused regardless of where he is ministering. He takes his mission extremely seriously and never makes it a trivial pursuit.

The book records a lifetime of staying true to one's calling, true to the Spirit's leading, and true to the original prophetic voice, rather than modifying it at every new twist and turn in the road. He refers to his life as riding Huckleberry Finn's raft – as his life journey has been one challenge and adventure after another. Each day is full of surprises and unknowns as he continues to pursue his kingdom mandate as an apostolic father who has traveled in over 80 countries.

In 1972, when we were landing in Dacca, Bangladesh, looking out the window of the plane, he said, "This is the fulfillment of a vision I received as a teenager." He told me that the landscape and topography were just as he had seen them in the vision. The nation had just been decimated by war with Pakistan where millions lost their lives. I felt that I was travelling with a New Testament apostle right out of the pages of the Bible.

This story has been repeated over and over again throughout his life, as this book will reveal. Moses has diligently followed the prophetic word just as the wise men followed the star from nation to nation.

As a man on a mission, he has always been fearless and willing to take whatever risks necessary and this is evidenced by all of his travels into communist countries where the threat of arrest and imprisonment was a constant reality.

Moses is extremely comfortable with witnessing to people in every setting. They are always drawn to him, want to hear his message, and will listen out of respect whether they agree or not.

This book is not only inspirational, but also instructional. It reveals the heart of a true apostolic father and his constant care and concern for the hundreds of relationships with ministers and churches that he has developed, trained, and mentored over the years.

This is a priceless resource and a library of information from a man privileged to experience the majority of the revivals that transpired during the twentieth century. The *Chronicles of Moses* is a recommended "must read" which I am delighted to endorse.

> Dr. David R. Kiteley
> Pastor Emeritus
> Shiloh Church, Oakland, California

Table of Contents

Introduction

"Be very careful never to forget what you have seen the Lord do for you, do not let these things escape from your mind as long as you live! And be sure to pass them on to your children and your grandchildren." [2]

It has been my joy, along with my precious wife Betty, to share these truths with our children, grandchildren, and great grandchildren as well as our many adopted children in the Lord. This is my legacy; and my prayer is that all of our descendants and many others will be blessed as they read of the gracious mercies of our God and the fulfillment of His Word to His servant Moses. I feel somewhat like Dr. Luke addressing his "most excellent Theophilus." (The name means "friend of God" or "God-lover.")

"Forasmuch as many have taken in hand to set forth in order a declaration of those things which are most surely believed among us, even as they delivered them unto us, which from the beginning were eyewitnesses and ministers of the word." [3]

It seemed good to me also to write to you an orderly account that you may know the certainty of those things which have transformed my life and marked my sixty-six years of following Jesus. I am constantly reminded and somewhat restrained by the wise words of Solomon.

"The preacher sought acceptable words, even to write down rightly words of truth or correct sentiment. The words of the wise are like prodding goads and firmly fixed in the mind like nails are the collected sayings which proceed from one Shepherd...of the making of books there is no end, and much study is a weariness of the flesh. Let us hear the conclusion of the whole matter: fear God, and keep His commandments: for this is the whole duty of man." [4]

---

2 Deuteronomy 4:9
3 Luke. 1:1-2
4 Ecclesiastes 12:10-13 The Amplified Bible

It is my prayer that as you peruse these pages you will be inspired to follow Jesus whole-heartedly. If you have not surrendered your life to Jesus Christ as Lord (Master and Owner), I pray that you will make that decision now. I am specifically writing to you who have a heart to pursue the call and purpose of God in your life. You may feel "disconnected" like millions of others who have gone a.w.o.l. I believe the greatest revival of all times will be the gathering of millions who are not "plugged in" to any church anywhere. I urge you to realize that you did not choose your ministry calling but that He chose you. He is the chooser and you are the "choosee." He also has ordained you that you should be fruitful and that your fruit should remain.[5] Listen for His call.

When I started my journey with Jesus I had several occasions where I saw myself in a vision. (It's the old guys who are to dream dreams according to the Prophet Joel. I still receive visions.) I would see myself floating down a very wide stream on something like a small raft. I suppose it would resemble a scene from Huckleberry Finn's adventures. Sometimes the waters were placid, and my little raft drifted smoothly with the current. There were other times  when I would come to the "rapids" to be shaken up by the turbulence of the times. I learned even most recently that I am to quit trying to control the storm or to determine the outcome! Jesus was always with me on my little raft. Then the Lord would order a "Selah," a rest stop. This was a time to pull over to the shore, recalibrate my compass, and await new orders. When I was refreshed and ready to sail on the Lord would thrust me on to my destination. I felt accelerated by the current of God's purposes and confident in my association with the Captain of our salvation.

---

[5] John 15:16

The fact that God could take an obscure Hungarian-Canadian thirteen-year-old and call him into ministry still amazes me. I actually finished the eighth grade, but in our family and in our country an eighth grade education meant that it was time to go to work. I thank the Lord for allowing me to get my G.E.D. later in life. Through one of my sons in the faith, Peter Snyder, I received an honorary Doctorate of Education from Wenshan Teachers College in Yunan Province, China, where I had the great privilege of lecturing. (My degree was made in China.) While I had never enrolled in a Bible college or seminary I have had the honor of helping to establish and teach in Bible schools in America and in various countries of the world. My education really came through the school of hard knocks, real life experiences, and through so much of God's grace and favor. I learned to bear His yoke in my youth.

God has sovereignly set me on the path of life that "no vulture's eye has ever seen."[6] This same Lord who called me by name declared to me prophetically that He would be faithful to give me the covenant promises He made to Abraham.[7] Those promises were indelibly inscribed on my heart and became the driving motivation and assurance for my lifelong journey.

From my earliest days of walking on this journey I began to see the awesome fulfillment of that heavenly vision that had captured my teen-age heart. What I am about to share with you in these "Chronicles" is meant to inspire you, to steel your nerves, and to fuel your faith, causing you to move on to your destination and the fulfillment of God's plan and purpose for your life. You can recapture the inexplicable joy of following Jesus and make your own calling and election sure. The pathway to heaven is simple. Make the first turn to the right and keep going straight.

Robert Frost wrote about "two roads diverged: I took the one less traveled." Jesus taught us to choose this narrow pathway to eternal life. That path is straight and narrow, but

---

[6] Job 28:7
[7] Genesis 12:1-3

it is not congested. Remember Paul's admonition to the believers in Rome.

"For God's gifts and His call are irrevocable. [He never withdraws them when once they are given, and He does not change His mind about those to whom He gives His grace or to whom He sends His call." [8]

Oswald Chambers said: God gives us our vision on the mountain top, then leads us into the valley to "mold" us (or as he says, to beat us) into the shape of it! All the promises of God are yes and amen to you. Don't ever let anyone steal your vision or rob you of your dream of a sweet eternal reward. Don't let any man take your crown.[9]

Highway 66

I am going to be transparent and even vulnerable in sharing with you the treasures of my heart that have accumulated over these sixty-six years of traveling the pathway which I think of as "The Acts of an Apostolic Journey," giving all the glory to Him who called me into His service.

"O God, You have taught me from my youth: and hitherto have I declared Your wondrous works. Yes, even when I am old and grey-headed, O God, forsake me not, [but keep me alive] until I have declared Your mighty strength to [this] generation, and Your might and power to all that are to come." [10]

This Pilgrim's Progress

As a boy I identified with John Bunyan's *Pilgrim's Progress*, a legendary book that my parents first read to me in Hungarian. I was inspired by reading it many times later in life. I discovered hideous monsters lurking in the shadows, giants of despair that would love to trap me in "Doubting Castle", or drown me in the "Slew of Despond." But up, oh valiant Pilgrim! "Run, John, run! The law

---

[8] Romans 11:29 The Amplified Bible
[9] Revelation 3:11
[10] Psalm 71:17-18

15

demands, but gives us neither feet nor hands. Far better news the Gospel brings, it bids me fly and gives me wings!"

We are already declared to be more than conquerors through Christ.[11] We don't have to worry about tomorrow. God is already there. God has never seemed to use a man in history because he had arrived, but because he was willing to go somewhere with God.

To begin a journey worthy of its destination you must remember that ability is what you are capable of doing; motivation determines what you do; but it is your attitude that determines how well you do it. So never let habit freeze you at your present level. Remember, the good old days are just ahead!

Yes you can! Millions of victorious believers who have blazed the trail before us surround us now like a great cloud of witnesses. Their names are indelibly inscribed in the "Who's Who" list of heaven. The Royal Leader of our faith is Jesus Christ Himself, who for the joy set before Him endured the cross, despised (counted as nothing) the shame, rejection, and even betrayal. He saw the first fruits of Calvary hanging before Him on the third cross. Jesus is the author and the finisher of our faith. That which He began in you He will finish. So do not be weary in well doing.

"Cast not away your confidence which has great recompense of reward."[12]

Hold on to that ticket, because you're going to have to present it to the conductor when you come out of your tunnel of despair!

---

[11] Romans 8:17
[12] Hebrews 10:32-35

Tell Me the Old, Old Story

My wife Betty and I have six children (One son is in heaven.) and nineteen grandchildren. (Two of them are in heaven.) At this writing we have five great granddaughters. When our children and grandchildren were small one or two would often crawl up on my lap and say, "Tell me a story." It was always a delight to share something old or something new with these marvelous offspring of ours. Occasionally one would ask for a "scary" story.

I would sometimes darken my countenance and lower my voice, almost to a low whisper. "It was a dark and cool Canadian night. My brothers and I were sound asleep in our upstairs barracks. Some of us were awakened by the sounds of shuffling and scraping near the wooden outside stairway. Closer and closer came the sounds. We saw a small flash of light that quickly died out. A moment later there was another, and then another. Curly first heard the creak of the bottom stair. Someone or something was coming out of the darkness. We saw another flash of light. We listened for another creak of the board. It was getting closer. Finally Bill turned on the porch light. It was our neighbor, 'Old Jack.' He was lighting matches and dropping them on the ground as he came staggering over to our place in a drunken stupor."

It wasn't long before I heard, "Stop it, Grandpa!" At that point I would share a more edifying story. How I cherish those memories of our devotions together as a family. We all love a story that ends well. And that is what I propose to tell, something old and something new, or as the amplified text says, "The fresh as well as the familiar."[13]

---

[13] Matthew 13.52

The Greatest Story Ever Told

My story, like yours, is more accurately the account of His grace and goodness working through this yielded vessel to accomplish His purposes. I have learned from my very early days that grown folks also love a good story. I have told and retold many excerpts of my journey with Jesus, usually weaving them into the message that the Lord had me deliver in many places, and oftentimes with the aid of an interpreter. You see, my journey has led me into about eighty countries and a myriad of cultures. Each group had been taught a distinct worldview including varying combinations of truth and error. With each group I have sought to leave a deposit of spiritual truth, sowing the seed that would grow in the good soil of sincere hearts and produce an abundant harvest of souls joyfully serving Jesus in His eternal kingdom.

Many of the hearers around the world were spiritual babes that needed a fresh supply of the milk of the Word. Others required meat, as they were more mature believers; emerging ministers that were hungry for the deeper things of God. It was always my intent to leave them stronger and more intensely hungry for God. Jesus is my compelling story.

After many years of prodding by our peers and parishioners I am now responding with a sincere heart to share my life's message. I am praying that as I muse, and as the fire burns, my heart will overflow with a good theme as I recite my composition concerning the King.

"O Lord let my tongue be the pen of a ready (skillful) writer." [14]

So prayerfully I proceed, ever conscious that every good thing in me is by His grace. I seek to readily reflect any and all the glory to Him who called me into His wonderful service.

---

[14] Psalm 45:1

In my family there were nine boys. To the delight of all the tenth and final sibling was a girl. I was the seventh in line. My father, Frank Vegh, had immigrated from Ersek Csanad, Hungary, on February 1, 1928, along with my two uncles who came to work in Windsor, Ontario, Canada. My mother, Juliana Vegh, along with her first three sons and their two aunts (Lydia and Irene) arrived about ten months later. They traveled through Cherbourg, France, on the Cunard line, docking in Halifax Harbor, Nova Scotia, Canada. There they boarded the Canadian National train bound for Windsor with their large "buchoos" (all their goods wrapped in great sheets that they carried on their heads). My Aunt Lydia kept looking out the window as they arrived at each railway stop, noticing the same sign reading "NO SMOKING." She said, "This is the largest city I have ever seen. We have traveled for more than three days on this train and we're still in "NO SMOKING!" After three long days and nights they finally arrived in Windsor, Ontario.

Mom and Dad and my brothers Frank, Louie and Joe were reunited as a family in nearby New Canaan, Essex County, where Dad had rented a little farm. A few years later they moved with their six children to a humble little home at 1091 Hickory Road in East Windsor.

Number Seven Arrives

I had quite a turbulent entrance into the Vegh family. It was early in the morning on April 21, 1933. Dad had already left for work when Mom started into labor. God sovereignly directed my paternal grandmother to come over and check on Mom. When she arrived, she immediately sensed something was wrong as she heard the anguish of my mother through the pains of her labor. Grandmother came to her bedside and found that I had already come forth but was barely breathing. The umbilical cord was wrapped tightly around my neck. I had already started to turn blue. Grandma ran to the kitchen and picked up a butcher knife.

Quickly and skillfully she cut me loose, turned me upside down, and soundly spanked my bottom. (She would do that many more times in my life.) As soon as I let out a good strong scream she pitched me into a clothes basket nearby and then tended to my mom.

The baby's cry was loud and piercing. It aroused our neighbor who came running over to our house. What was that wailing sound coming out of the clothes basket? Our good Hungarian neighbor was Mrs. Szabados (meaning Mrs. Freedom). She exclaimed "Jaj! It's little Mozes in the bulrushes!" That was the beginning of Moses Vegh. I was given no middle name. The name "Moses" in Hebrew means "drawn out" (of the water). This name was given to Moses by

Jaj! Mozes!

Pharaoh's daughter who adopted him. Végh in Hungarian means the "end." Perhaps that's why I had the recurring vision of me floating on my small barque which I shall call my little raft throughout these musings.

This was the beginning of a life that was miraculously spared; the genesis of a journey that has continued to unfold in ever increasing manifestations of God's grace. My early days happened to be during the height of the depression that had gripped the whole world. We did not know we were poor, (Everyone around us was poor.) but we were conscious of living under the shadow of the Almighty. My father was a diligent worker who provided the best he could for his expanding family. One day Dad was miraculously selected out of hundreds of men in an unemployment line to work for the Auto Light Company in Windsor. He later worked for the Ford Motor Company as a tool and die maker.

My Dad was a teaching elder (pastor) in the old Hungarian Nazarene Church where we all attended Sunday school and church for several years in Windsor, Ontario. My grandfather and great grandfather were also Hungarian Nazarene pastors back in the old country. It seems to me that my pastoral heritage goes all the way back to Abraham. Well, at least back to Moses.

Zolt Curly Bill Joe Lou Frank Jr. Dad Mom with Eddie on board Moses

Time to Move On

We soon outgrew our little home on Hickory Road. Dad bought an old shell of a house and had it moved about five miles to Tecumseh Road in East Windsor. Our fourteen hundred square foot home had a basement and a partial upstairs which was the "boy barracks." This humble home became the center of my life for at least fourteen years. We had a little garden, some chickens, and a cow, which our amazing mom utilized for most of our daily needs. She had a saying that a rock would make good soup if you put enough with it. Mom loved to grow poppies for the poppy seed cakes she would bake. Back during the war we did not know it was against the law to grow poppies. One day a brilliantly clad Canadian Mounted Policeman arrived at our door. He was carrying a clip board. Mom thought he was a boy scout selling apples for their troop outing. "No thanks, Honey," she said. But the "mountie" never smiled. He was on a mission to tear out her poppy plants because poppies were known to be used for making heroin. He accomplished his mission and mom shed some tears over her precious poppy seed loss. But Mom was resilient and versatile. She soon found other sources for her poppy-seed and walnut cakes.

Doctor Jesus Makes House Calls

We never knew what it was to have a doctor make house calls for any of us if we were sick. (There was one exception. Every two years or so Dr. George came to our house with a new baby brother. I think he brought him in a cardboard box.) Whenever we were sick Mom would pray the prayer of faith and God would heal us. However, if any of us were really sick for any duration Mom would fix a place on the living room couch, white sheets, pillows, and a place where the siblings could come and" ooh" and "ahh." It was mostly out of envy for the "tender loving care" we might be receiving. Oh, yes, and she made delicious chicken soup (which seemed to cure any disease)!

I had an intense desire for that TLC I had witnessed. I heard of an epidemic of mumps that had broken out in my third grade class. My best friend, Billy, had developed a severe case. I went over to him and begged him to share the blessing. "Please, Billy, blow on me and rub my neck. I must catch your mumps." I did! I arrived home for lunch, all excited and expecting to activate Mom's emergency room procedure.

"Mom, I have a note from the school nurse that says I have the mumps, and I am quarantined to stay in bed for ten days. Please get the couch ready and kill that chicken. I am ready for my ten days of TLC."

Momma was a typical Hungarian Christian mother. She always had a radiant expression of the joy of the Lord on her face. She typically wore a white apron while cooking, and she often wiped her brow with it. She was a worshipper who would sing while she cooked on the stove or bent over the wash board, always giving praise continually to the Lord. I loved her dearly, but that day I did not want her near me.

She said, "Oh, come on, Honey. Just let me feel your mumps."

"No way. I know you, Mom. These are my mumps and I am ready for my ten days of TLC!"

She lovingly reached out and drew me into her ample bosom. She gently stroked my neck and prayed softly, and the mumps were gone! I was angry and disappointed. Mom said, "Young people today are so nervous and irrigated!" (At that point she had not quite mastered the English language.) Back to school I went.

I remember another time when I was very sick with a high fever and strep throat. I was about nine years old. Mom had made me comfortable on the couch. She was sitting by me, singing and praying. I was delirious but suddenly I had a vision of heaven. I saw many children playing by the river of life. I especially recognized Samuel the prophet who was now a young boy in my vision. We talked and walked by the River of Life. It was a beautiful flowing river with the Tree of Life on either side, arching over the stream with twelve kinds of fruit, and the leaves were for the healing of the nations. I was narrating everything I saw to Mom who was weeping and praising God by my couch. When I returned from my heavenly vision I was completely healed and hungry. Mom had me repeat that experience to her many times. That vision was indelibly printed on my heart and mind. Heaven is real. She seemed to have a special bonding with me, and, of course, I felt I was very special to her also. I know she truly loved all of her ten children, but my mother made me feel especially loved. I suspect that all of my siblings felt the same way.

Life in the Vegh Family

There never was a dull moment at the Vegh house with ten children, my parents, and the many guests that came by. Our life revolved around our family meals, with Dad praying before and after each meal. I remember that each child had his place, according to his age, around our great kitchen table. We had "coffee soup" for our breakfast that we ladled onto the hearty pieces of bread in our bowls. At dinnertime I remember eagerly waiting for the plate of chicken being passed around clockwise and viewing the diminishing chicken as it finally arrived at my place. I usually got the piece that went over the fence last. Mom would stand over us and often say, "I am just feasting on you" as she managed to get a few bites off the backbone or the feet. Mom said these were her favorite pieces.

We had to arise very early in the morning if we wanted to find a pair of matching socks. Our clothes were usually hand-me-downs. They were clean, but not always in fashion. We each had our chores to do. We would milk the cow, feed the chickens, sweep, mop, and even help with dishes. I loved to help Mom bake and cook.

We all shared one bathroom. Our sister, Vi, was the caboose on the Vegh train. The day she was born Mom fainted for joy at finally having a girl. I expected to be immediately liberated from doing kitchen chores. No more dishes! No more washing clothes! That was one vision that did not come to pass. What a surprise it was to have to wait until my sister Vi grew up to enjoy her long-awaited help. She did become a dynamic dishwasher, but not before I had completed what seemed to me to be a lifetime's worth of KP.

A Dynamic Discovery

We grew up with a father who had a very strict holiness upbringing, so he did not believe in having a radio. He thought that radios were the devil's instruments. My older, wiser, and enterprising brothers secretly built a crystal set radio with a long copper line antenna stretched across our "barracks" upstairs. We could only receive one signal, and that was from CKLW in Windsor, Ontario, a Mutual Broadcasting clear channel station.

One Sunday I snuck upstairs to listen to our radio, and there was Dad hunched over the table. He was listening on the earphones to the Old Fashioned Revival Hour Quartet singing, "Give the winds a mighty voice; Jesus Saves! Jesus Saves!" The great Charles E. Fuller was speaking on that broadcast. Dad was in tears as he heard the glorious singing and the sound preaching of the Word. Wow! Something good has come out of this "evil" thing. Praise the Lord!

I remember going with Dad down old Wyandotte Street in Windsor to a used furniture store. There we found an old Atwaterkent cabinet radio. This marvelous piece of furniture became our family focal point in the living room. We would gather each evening to listen to the news narrated by men like Gabriel Heater, Lowell Thomas, Paul Harvey, and many other seasoned reporters. Then we would tune in to some exciting drama stories. We heard ghost stories on Sunday night, along with the "Mummers" and "The Shadow." It was fun growing up in a large Christian family. Dad and Mom found great solace in the daily religious broadcasts. Bishop C. L. Morton's Sunday afternoon broadcasts over CKLW became our Sunday nourishment. Bishop Morton was a noted black pastor with the Church of God in Christ. He became a lifelong friend and mentor. He was a very gifted preacher. He also happened to be the father of ten children, some of whom are in the ministry today.

The Vegh Family with all Ten Children

Chapter Two

Uncle Alex Arrives

A new chapter opened to our family when Uncle Alex and Aunt Irene arrived one day in 1945 with their eight children from British Columbia. I remember seeing them drive up in a 1924 model T Ford truck[15] loaded with all their stuff. They were simple people, but they resonated with the joyful message of the spiritual blessing they had received in British Columbia. Most of the family moved in with us. (Can you say, "Wait in line for the bathroom?") Fortunately we were able to send a few of them down the street to Grandma's house.

Uncle Alec readily began to share with my father his newfound joy in the baptism of the Holy Spirit. Dad was a staunch member of the Hungarian Nazarene church, but he was very curious to discover what it was that made Uncle Alex so happy. Dad finally consented to go to a Pentecostal meeting held in the home of some Hungarian friends. While he was in this meeting he witnessed the folks worshipping and lifting up their hands in praise. Dad came home and thought, "I'm going to try this." He quietly raised his hands while lying on the front room couch. Suddenly the Holy Spirit came on him and he was baptized in the Holy Ghost! We came running in to find him speaking in a heavenly language. We thought he might have had a stroke, but he had discovered that river that Jesus spoke about in John 7:37-39.

Soon Dad was excommunicated from the Nazarene Church. Things were never the same in our home. Dad was on fire for the Lord. He and Uncle Alex and a few Hungarian believers bought a store-front building on Parent Avenue in Windsor, Ontario. My brothers and I helped clean out the remains of an old grocery store and quickly renovated the Parent Avenue Full Gospel Mission. Our life revolved around this humble little mission, a haven for so many rescued souls.

---

[15] think: Beverly Hillbillies

Salvation is a Household Word [16]

Mom's intercession for my older brother Bill had prevailed. He was gloriously healed of tuberculosis and a crushed foot that had been injured in the Merchant Marines. One day Bill had a powerful encounter with Jesus while he was watching a movie in a local theater. The movie was making mockery of Jesus and the Gospel. Bill was deeply convicted by the Holy Spirit and right there he gave his heart to the Lord. He was dramatically changed and immediately set about to witness to his old friends and to as many as he could find on the streets of Windsor. Often he would bring a drunken man home. He would bathe, clothe and feed him, and then introduce him to Jesus. Soon he was preaching, singing, and leading the worship in the little mission on Parent Avenue. Bill began to intercede for all of his brothers and friends, spending many long nights out in the country fields walking and praying. During this time he made me his special target.

Dear Lord Save Moses!

Although my Mom, Dad, and Grandma had taught me to pray (both in English and Hungarian) I still needed to be born again. Bill did not tell me that he was praying specifically for me and that he had made a covenant with the Lord for my life. He set a deadline for my conversion to be within the next two weeks.[17] During that time Bill was fasting and praying for my salvation. Bill had made a deal with my folks that they were not to disturb me or discipline me for anything for two weeks. During this time the devil made me a special instrument of torment to my brother Bill and to the rest of my family. Bill kept a sweet spirit even though I tormented him, and I was getting very uneasy because no one seemed to respond to my obnoxious behavior. On the last night of the two weeks Bill preached his heart out in the Sunday evening service. I sat in the back of the church resisting the pull of the Holy Spirit and was so

---

[16] Acts 16:31
[17] That was in November of 1946.

relieved when the service was over. Little did I know that Bill had less than twenty-four hours to see a change in me before the two week deadline.

The next day was November 19, 1946. I attended a meeting at the mission with a group of mostly young people. After the meeting Bill was driving some of us home in his 1929 Durant. I was seated in the back seat by my cousin, Betty. (She was a fervent intercessor.) At the city limits Bill stopped the car and announced that anyone in the car who did not want to stop and pray should get out. (It was the last city bus stop.) I was the only one among the five of us who did not really want to pray, but I was not at all interested in walking home.

By that point I was miserably under conviction and hoping that they would not notice me huddled in the corner of the back seat. I wanted to sit and quietly wait for them to finish praying. Bill pulled off the main road into the Malden Road bush and all four of them began to pray fervently. Heaven responded. Suddenly into that darkness of night I saw the Lord in a vision. He came toward me in splendor, clothed in a shining white robe with a gold sash and walking down a long red carpet. I saw Jesus walking toward me and there were trumpeters on either side of this great red carpet which led right into my heart. As Jesus came into my heart I saw dark demons scattering and Jesus mounted the throne room of my heart. He has been there ever since.

I shall never forget the joyful expression on the faces of those in the car as the glory of the Lord radiated around us in the car. We were all weeping and praising God for His wonderful salvation and just in time, for Moses was genuinely born again. I looked up in this visible glory and saw the little clock on the mirror. It was five minutes before midnight; five minutes before the two weeks when Bill's contract with the Lord was up. The Lord is faithful. He may seem slow, but He is never late.

I remember the joy of coming home right after my glorious experience early in the morning and walking in to mother's room to tell her and Dad of my wonderful experience. Mom got up and joyfully worshiped with me and

28

reminded me that God had a plan and purpose for my life. After a few hours sleep I awakened, and Bill told me that we must go back to the mission and tarry for the baptism of the Holy Spirit. He reminded me that this was part of the "Peter package" we had read about in Acts 2:38. I was very willing to go and soon we were at the mission. We began to pray fervently, and at about 6:00 p.m. several young people joined us.

It was about 10:00 that night as we were all praying that I had a vision of Jesus standing in a river and beckoning me to come to Him. I heard Him say, "Are you willing to follow me into the waters of baptism?" I said, "Yes Lord," and immediately I was filled with the Holy Spirit. I began to speak in a language that I had not learned. All those around me, including some of my cousins, were worshiping and praising God. Bill baptized me in the Detroit River soon after that. The water was bitterly cold, but what a glorious day! The "old Moses" was buried. A new man arose with a "circumcised heart."[18]

I basked in this glorious flow for many days. I could not understand why so many people where testifying about hard times, trials, temptations, and all kinds of conflict. Little did I know that I was riding on the faith of those around me. This spiritual and emotional "honeymoon" lasted a few months, and then I was introduced to my adversary, the devil, through many tests and trials. The Lord graciously caused me to learn and know His mighty power over the enemy of my soul, and that by submitting to God I could resist the devil and he would flee from me.

How I Met Jabez

One day while I was praying on my knees by my bed in our upstairs barracks with my Bible opened I asked the Lord why it was that I had been so sad since my early youth. I had been given to crying and weeping at the slightest provocation. During our early years my brothers could easily bring me to tears, and they often did. I really wanted to fight,

---

[18] Colossians 2:11

but I would quickly melt with deep sorrow instead. My brothers and their friends nicknamed me "Sad Sack," or just plain "Sack." I earnestly prayed for the Lord to set me free from this sorrow. I was born again and filled with the Spirit, but I still remained under a cloud of sorrow.

Chronicles Hold the Key

The Holy Spirit instructed me to open my Bible to First Chronicles chapter one, and I read it carefully. This was like instructing me to go to the courthouse and read the entrees in the archives. "How boring," I thought. I began reading in chapter one, and after about 140 verses of "begats and begots" I discovered the two verses in chapter four that gave us all we know about a character named Jabez. Right in the middle of the genealogy litany the Holy Ghost dropped in a short but powerful biographical sketch that had a powerful impact on me.

Of course this was long before our friend Bruce Wilkerson wrote his book about those three verses. Who was this guy who was more honorable than his brothers? His mother gave him the name Jabez (meaning sorrowful, or "Sad Sack") because she had borne him in pain. By naming her son in response to her own difficulties the mother put a stigma on her son that had an effect on his life. Only the grace of God could break the curse of that negative name. Jabez received that grace because he looked to the Lord for his help and called out with gratitude and humility.

And Jabez called on the God of Israel saying, "Oh that You would bless me indeed, and enlarge my territory or my borders, and that Your hand would be with me, and that you would keep me from evil, that I may not cause pain!" So God granted him what he requested.[19]

It seemed like heaven opened to me. God gave me the assurance of Jabez. The Lord showed me that my sorrow had been transferred to me by my mother who apparently suffered grief while I was in her womb. I cried out to the Lord and He heard me. I prayed the prayer of Jabez and it

---

[19] 1 Chronicles 4:9-10 The Amplified Bible

30

worked. I was totally set free from my sorrow and refreshed in the Holy Spirit. My mom noticed the change and the joy and radiance on my face and she asked me what happened. I said, "Mom, I am no longer bound by sorrow. I have the garments of joy and praise and I am set free. I have discovered God's word of deliverance for me!"

"Now Mom, please tell me what you were going through while you carried me in your womb?"

"Who told you? How did you find out?" she asked.

"The Lord led me to Jabez in His word and showed me that I was born in sorrow as Jabez was. He led me to pray the prayer of Jabez and I was completely set free. I prayed and my sorrow now is turned to perpetual joy. Please, Mom, tell me about your experience when you were carrying me."

Mom began to weep as she recounted the days of her sorrow. She told me that she and Dad experienced marital problems during that pregnancy, and the wounds were very deep in her heart. We both discovered through God's word the powerful effects of the transfer of sorrow. Another similar Biblical account was Jacob's wife Rachel[20] who was actually under a curse of death. In her last moments she sought to transmit her sorrow to the son to whom she was giving birth. She called him "Ben-Oni" (son of my sorrow), but Jacob did not let her do it. "Rachel, you're my very favorite wife, and I love you. But I will not put a negative label on this son." Jacob called his name Benjamin (son of my right hand).

As I shared with Mom in those wonderful moments how God had revealed this to me, a beautiful release came to both of us! We both began singing a song of a soul set free. This was also a moment of precious bonding with my mother. That delightful affinity in the spirit was to play a very important part in my ministry in the days to come. I cherish the memories of that day that I met Jabez who has become my lifelong friend.

Little did I know that so many years later I would be writing about my "Jabez" experience. Everything must

---

[20] Genesis 31:18-32

become specific before it becomes dynamic. In my ongoing walk with Jesus I found that He has a way of taking seriously anyone that takes His word seriously. His word was and is my daily delight and has opened a great door of hope and opportunity. Now follow me on my little raft and we will discover new and marvelous adventures.

Moses meets Jabez

Chapter Three

The School of the Holy Spirit

Shortly after my conversion at age thirteen my cousin Elmer[21] and I decided to travel to Toronto, Ontario. It was very cold and just a few days after Christmas in 1946. We had very limited resources as we hitchhiked on Old Highway 2 in a blizzard. We prayed for someone to pick us up. We got a lift to Ingersoll, Ontario, and there it seemed that no one was willing to give two boys a ride. We prayed for the Lord to help us make it to Toronto or back to Windsor. At that point we just wanted some respite from the freezing cold!

Finally at about 2:00 in the morning we were picked up by a semi-trailer truck driver who delivered us to Dundas Street in Toronto to the home of some of our old family friends. It was here in the Sabolski home that God brought new revelation and direction to my life. The Sabolskis owned a large apartment house with a storefront church on the main floor. I was asked to stay with them for a few weeks. Their own teenage son, Adam, had recently been killed in a car accident. Mrs. Sabolski took me in as her own son. She was a wonderful mom to me for a short time. Ten or so Bible school students rented rooms upstairs in their large home. We spent many nights in prayer together, and several of those students became prominent leaders in the Canadian Assemblies of God in the years to come.

One winter evening in February, 1947, I came in late from my job of delivering groceries on a toboggan. I was cold, wet, and hungry. As I entered the hallway that led to Mrs. Sabolski's kitchen, where my soup was waiting, I could hear the cries of an intercessor coming from the little store front church next to the kitchen where I was sitting. She was praying fervently in the spirit in a heavenly language.

I felt constrained by the Lord to go into the meeting. As I entered the side door the presence of the Lord overwhelmed me. In a moment I found myself prostrate in the entrance. Then the young lady who was praying in tongues began to

---

[21] Elmer was saved about the same time as I was and was two years older.

prophesy concerning the call of God on my life. She did not know me nor did she know that I was in the building, but as she spoke the Word of the Lord I could see everything she was saying in a vision. God kept asking me prophetically if I were willing to go and preach the gospel to all the nations that I saw revolving on a large colored globe of the world.

"Yes Lord!" I responded. "I will go. I will preach and I will tell the wonderful story of Jesus and His love." That vision has sustained me for all these years. It is still being fulfilled and I know the Lord watches over His Word to perform it!

While in Toronto I had the privilege of being in a fellowship at the Stone Church where Hugh McAllister was the pastor. One cold Friday night old "Daddy Chambers" arrived and he was invited to preach in the youth service that I attended. He was a legendary preacher who was on his way to Florida at the time. This venerable saint preached with great anointing about the "double portion" Elisha requested when he received Elijah's mantle. I was among the many who filled the altar that night, and revival broke out. Brother Chambers announced that he was directed by the Lord to stay. He continued for six weeks preaching every night. The Lord allowed me to meet some of God's outstanding spiritual leaders in Canada at that time including: J. Oswald Smith (a missions legend), Maxwell White, Winston Nunes, Tommy Johnson, Lori Price, and Hope Smith, who had a great impact on my life.

In the spring of 1947 I returned to Windsor and settled back at home for a season. The harbingers of revival were in the air. In addition to serious Bible study and prayer daily we were being fed spiritually by *The Golden Grain,* a monthly publication of Dr. Charles Price, and also with books by E. W. Kenyon and John G. Lake. During these days we were also introduced to the ministry of William Branham. We later visited his home and met his family. W. J. "Ern" Baxter from Vancouver, B.C., Canada, was traveling with Brother Branham as his Bible teacher during those years. Ern Baxter and I became very close friends and shared many years of fellowship and ministry before he was promoted to heaven in 1993.

Meanwhile, back home our little group of young believers at the mission in Windsor set our hearts to fast and pray for the restoration of all that God had spoken through His prophets.[22] We felt constrained to have someone on their knees around the clock. My brother, Bill, Dan Miller (my dear friend and fellow evangelist), and I would spend rotating hours on our knees, interceding for a mighty ingathering of the harvest. The fires of Holy Ghost zeal burned in our hearts. Miracles of healing, deliverances, and salvation were abundant. We often conducted street meetings in the city of Windsor where we all, as young converts, had to take our turns testifying and sharing the Gospel. Many precious souls were saved in those days as we continued on our journey with Jesus. God was getting me ready for that which He had already prepared for me.

Learning to Bear the Yoke

During that time my brother Bill had invited me to travel with him to a mission on the Muncy Indian Reservation near London, Ontario. It was in the spring of 1947 that Bill and I arrived at the old Half Moon Church. We had driven through snow, slush, and mud roads in a friend's '37 Ford. The primitive church building was about one hundred years old and was made of huge logs with split logs for benches. There was no electricity, so we used pump-up gas lamps that lasted for about two hours. The Lord did a mighty work during those hours.

The Lord gave us His favor. Bill and I sang and preached and the Lord gave the increase. My first evangelistic text was Romans 9:33.

---

[22] Acts 3:19-21

As it is written, behold I lay in Zion a stumbling stone and a rock of offense: and whosoever believes in Him shall not be ashamed.

This text formed the cornerstone of my life's message. I learned early in my journey with Jesus not to despise the day of small beginnings. This was the word of the Lord to Zerubbabel when he was told that it was not by might nor by power but by the Spirit of the Lord.[23]

During this meeting, Chief Percy Wadlow and his whole family of thirty-seven people responded to the Word and were saved. I remember our offering was about $2.18. But the dividends kept coming! By now Bill recognized the call of God on my life and willingly mentored me. He invited me along to many subsequent meetings.

Our next stop was at the Six Nations Indian Reserve at Oshweken, near Brantford, Ontario. There God met us in a mighty way. On our first night in this very scary place we were met by the witch doctor of the tribe and her entourage. She was a tall, ugly, snaggle-toothed woman who was intent on running us out of the village. I learned very quickly to plead the blood of the Lamb. After much prayer some reinforcements of believers from the Brantford Gospel Tabernacle arrived. The enemy was routed and we had a glorious revival!

After the witch-doctor and her clan left the building where we were staying Bill and I settled down in a little bedroom in the back of the church. We slept on a straw bed that smelled like a corn crib. On the wall was a little faded memory verse. This verse was indelibly inscribed in my heart.

"The Lord is good, a strong hold in the day of trouble; and he knows them that trust in Him." [24]

---

[23] Zechariah 4:6
[24] Nahum 1:7

We had to pray over everything we ate. We got by on a very meager supply. We had a can of peas, a can of pears, a little tea, and some bread. I believe we also had a few eggs. It was bitterly cold outside. We found about three feet of snow piled up around our 1931 model "A" Ford. That old Ford also served as our ice-box. Incidentally, that car would often run for miles with the gas gauge registering "empty" as Bill prayed for divine provision. Often we had no money for gas, but we did have faith. One night we received a plate of boiled chicken just before church began. I stored it on the floorboard of our car hoping to have a feast after church. When we retrieved it, we found it was soaked with gasoline, dripping from the leaking gas tank above. Some neighborhood dogs had a feast that night!

Our old potbelly stove had burned-out grates in it so it was a challenge to get a fire going. Of course, we had very little fuel to burn. I actually shaved off some of the rustic door trim for kindling. This was our boot camp where God taught us great and wonderful lessons about prayer, revival, and His abundant supply.

These lessons have sustained us over the years. Many young lives were changed in those early days of evangelism by the power of the Gospel of Jesus Christ. Nobody told us it was hard, so we just kept on going! I had my first experience with preaching on the radio in Brantford, Ontario, with Pastor Gus Porter of the Indian Reserve Church. They always opened their program with the same line of a song: "If you really have a blessing you will shine!" I don't think it reached around the world, but it was a great experience for a fourteen year old preacher!

The Lord also gave us favor with the little Full Gospel Tabernacle in nearby Brantford, Ontario with Pastor John Gibson and his dear congregation. We made lifelong friendships with many of these precious folks, including Bill and Marg Collins and their family. To this day they are still some of our best friends.

I continued on in that area preaching to the Indians for a season. Since finances were very meager on the reserve I got a job for a while working at the Watson Underwear knitting mill in Brantford, Ontario. My boss (a good Baptist brother) noticed that I was frequently distracted from my job. I was reading my Bible and praying constantly in the Spirit. The seven knitting machines that I was supposed to be tending often broke down while I was sitting on the floor with my Bible. My supervisor, Harvey, graciously advised me to tend to my job or just leave and go preach the Gospel. I decided to leave. I headed back to Windsor and continued in my quest to grow deeper in the Lord.

Chapter Four   *The Latter Rain*

We experienced a significant climate change in our early days at the Parent Street Mission.[25] Our little group of mostly young believers began in earnest seeking a fresh outpouring of God's Spirit. We were already apprised of God's intervention in sending men like William Branham into the world. He was the forerunner in a wave of faith healers who were coming on the scene at that time.

We read in the Bible that we are to ask the Lord for rain in the time of the latter rain.[26] The prophet Hosea said, that the Lord Himself would come to us as the "rain" the early and the latter rain.[27] We also were instructed to break up our fallow ground.[28] We lived in the Word continually. We felt a burning hunger for the supernatural outpouring and manifestation gifts of the Holy Spirit.

It is significant to note that the Lord spoke about the "early" rain and the "latter" rain. The early rain (Hebrew word, Moreh) means a "teacher of righteousness." God had sent an abundance of teaching on righteousness, or right standing with God and the restoration of the gifts. There was also clear preaching of the Gospel that brought genuine conviction and then spiritual conversion. I know some folks thought we were radical, but I remember altar calls when the whole church would come to the altar for more of God, for the infilling of the Holy Spirit, and for the renouncing of the sins of the flesh. This rain germinated the Gospel seed that had been sown.

The "latter rain" (Hebrew word, *Molquosh)* refers to a confirming rain that came to set the fruit of the harvest three months later. God promised to give us both rains in the same month.[29] We had come to a time of germination,

---

[25] 1947-1948
[26] Zechariah 1:10
[27] Hosea 6:1-3
[28] Hosea 10:12
[29] Joel 2:23

maturation, and fruition. This was actually a season of acceleration by association that is spoken of in Amos 9:11-13 "when the plowman would overtake the reaper."

We believed that surely this was the time for the Lord to restore all that the prophets have spoken of in the Bible. Leonard Ravenhill, in his book *Why Revival Tarries,* said, "Before God arises to shake the world, He must shake His church with some obscure truth." Many folks could not embrace what God was doing in those days, but we were confident that a season of refreshing was on the way; a season whose time had come.

We had heard the report of a dedicated group of Bible students who had been gathering in a Quonset hut on an abandoned air field in North Battleford, a suburb of Saskatoon, Saskatchewan, Canada. Something supernatural was happening with this unusual group. We heard of the phenomenal outpouring of God's spirit upon about seventy students and teachers who had set themselves apart to fast and pray and seriously seek the Lord for a restoration of the gifts of the Holy Spirit. They were given a special emphasis on the revelation of the five-fold ministry in the book of Ephesians.

Two teachers, Ernest and George Hawtin, were brothers who led the excursion into the vast dynamism that would be poured out on them. Spontaneous revelations came to them that led them deeper than they had ever been before. The stories of divine revelation and subsequent manifestations of the gifts of the Holy Spirit, including powerful healings and miracles, are now recorded history. These men of God didn't just have conferences on psychosomatic medicine. They healed the sick. They didn't just say their prayers. They really talked with God.

There was one instance when a group of these anointed men went to the local Catholic hospital and asked to pray for a man dying with cancer. He was already in a coma, and his face had a gaping hole eaten away by cancer. They simply laid hands on him in the name of Jesus and instantly he revived, and then he immediately asked for some breakfast. The Mother Superior was called. She said, "Oh, he is delusional. Go ahead and order his breakfast, but he can't eat or swallow." Witnesses there watched as the hole in his face began to fill in with healthy tissue and skin. He devoured the meal he received and asked for another plate! In a very short time the wound had healed completely. That man's healing was a powerful testimony to many of the power of God.

The rain was falling in abundance. On one occasion when they were praying for the "rain" they suddenly heard the sound of rain falling loudly and clearly on the roof of their metal Quonset hut. I have been told by very credible witnesses that someone ran out of the building to close the windows of his car. When he went out he was perplexed and amazed to see that the sky was clear. There was not a drop of physical rain! These and many other reports also fueled our passion to intercede for the restoration of the supernatural! I actually tried to apply for the North Battleford Bible School, but I was told that I was too young to attend.

At about this same time,[30] back in Windsor, a few of us young men were staying in the living quarters of the Parent Avenue Mission. We were fasting and praying and maintaining a 24/7 pray chain with at least one of us on our knees all the time. We began in earnest to intercede for all our families and friends to be saved.

Salvation Comes Home

The atmosphere in our home was changing as each of us, especially my mother, was praying and constantly admonishing one another to pray for our family members who were unsaved. My brothers Frank, Louie, Joe, Curly and Bill had all served in the various departments of military service. They all returned safely home after the war. I am convinced that their continued safety in that bloody conflict

---

[30] early in 1948

was the direct result of the prayer cover of my family members. Mom would listen to Pastor M.D. ("Mom") Beall on her radio every morning as she called "America to Your Knees." Myrtle Beall was a mighty intercessor who pioneered Bethesda Missionary Temple, a great church in Detroit, Michigan. Throughout World War II the church maintained a fervent prayer vigil for the dozens of young men from the church who were deployed to the battlefields of the world. Miraculously not one of their boys was killed in the war that claimed fifty-six million lives.

No matter how much my brothers indulged in the sinful vices of the world, often coming home quite inebriated, they always knelt by their bedside and prayed for fear that Jesus might come in the night and they would be left behind! Of course they had many of these experiences before most of them accepted Jesus and became involved in serving the Lord.

Discovering the Scarecrow

Having eight brothers and one sister who took time to play games with me and improvise exciting activities was a great joy. One of those adventures was "finding" watermelons in our neighbor's garden. Bill taught me that the biggest melons could be found in the darkest night by simply going to the scarecrow. This has been a very useful anecdote in my teaching ministry as I assure my fellow believers that Satan always places his "scarecrows" near God's greatest treasures. Spiritual treasures are ready to be received and enjoyed if we pursue them in faith with a focus on God and His purposes.

My brother Zolten and I were very close. He was just two years my senior. Zolt had a tender heart but was rather wild in his teenage years. Consequently Zolt was Bill's second target. Once we buried Dad's tractor in a deep ditch playing war games. Bill pleaded with the Lord and pledged that he, Zolt, and I would fast for a day if God would help us get the tractor out before Dad got home. God did help us and Zolt could hardly wait until sundown to end his fast. He was ready to start eating the candy bars he had stashed in his pocket. Zolt always thought ahead.

My brothers and I had so many delightful adventures over the years. Once our number five brother, Curly, punished our younger brother, Ed, (who was tormenting him and probably deserved it). Curley opened the "trap door" on Ed's long johns and branded his bottom by setting him on the hot Quebec gas heater in our barracks. Ed's screams brought Dad running upstairs. Dad gave us all the rod, but Ed bore the imprint "Quebec heater" on his rear for quite some time.

I had the joy of praying with my brothers over the years and ministering to them at various junctures of their lives. I have been honored to minister at our family funerals, beginning with our dad's funeral in 1988. I also administered the funerals of my brothers Curly, Bill, Frank and most recently Joe, who passed away on our 59th wedding anniversary, August 29, 2012. My oldest living brother, Lou, then passed away as I was writing this book. He died on December 16, 2012. He was almost ninety. I have four siblings left: Zolt, Ed, Bob, and our baby sister Violet Victoria Mary Vegh Rawlings. (Mom had a whole list of names for her long-desired daughter.) We just call her "Vi." Today I am so thankful to say we all are serving the Lord in various capacities.

We have enjoyed a rich legacy in the Lord by God's grace, notwithstanding the many heartaches and trials of each individual family. The prevailing faith that was imparted by our grandparents and our parents sustained us. The Lord continues to shape, sift, and correct each of us in a way that is compatible to His covenant promise to "keep that which we have committed unto Him against that day." As long as we are on this earth we will keep striving for His perfection to be wrought in us.

I recall the two large framed Scriptures, artistically printed both in Hungarian and in English that adorned our dining room wall. These words reverberate in our hearts almost daily. They were the words of Joshua 24:15.

"As for me and my house, we will serve the Lord."

Pursuing the Prophetic

In every new beginning there is a word. In your new beginnings you too shall hear a word. God is raising up a generation that will hear His voice, and the humble among them will be quick to respond. This generation will learn to be "voice activated." This was our greatest hunger and desire in our pursuit of the mighty gifts of the Lord. We learned to live by every "proceeding" word from the Lord. Often we would place the Bible on our table and just tremble at His word as we discovered it was more valuable than our necessary food. We found His word and we did eat it![31] Jeremiah declared,

"Thy words were found and I ate them, and Your word was to me the joy and the rejoicing of my heart; for I am called by Your name, O Lord of hosts."[32]

We had discovered the Word that had become flesh. Eugene Peterson's translation, *The Message*, says: *"The Word became flesh and blood and moved into the neighborhood."[33]* I believe He did move into my life in a very personal and dramatic way. Jesus is intensely real to my heart. He is my friend, my counselor, and my consoler. I believe this was the birthing of the whole concept of oral Bible training that in later years was picked up by our son, Marcus. Jesus gave us powerful word descriptions of His Father as He spoke in parables, or real life stories.[34]

---

31 Job 23:12
32 Jeremiah15:16
33 John 1:14
34 Matthew 13:34-35

We learned that God was not giving us the silent treatment and we were wired for sound. We would call upon Him and He would answer. We believed His word and embraced the voice of His prophets. We knew that we were living in the day of the "Voice of the Lord," and when we called on Him he would answer us and show us great and mighty things we did not know.[35] We began to desire and even covet spiritual gifts. We learned to discern our gifts, to develop what He gave us, and to deploy the gifts in season.[36] God wants us to be a prophetic community.

Another Journey on my Little Raft

During our time of hunger and quest for God and the prophetic we heard of a certain prophet who lived in Toledo, Ohio. One day my brother Bill suggested that five of us get in his 1930 Durant and drive to Ohio to visit the man. We were hungry to hear a

Moses and Bill Vegh
Granite City, 1948

word from the Lord. We felt that perhaps God would have a word for us through his prophet. Of course we didn't think it was necessary for us to phone ahead and set up an appointment. We assumed that if he were a true prophet he would surely know we were coming and would be waiting for us.

When we arrived in Toledo, I gave Bill my last quarter to call the prophet's home from a street pay phone. His wife answered and said the prophet was far away on a ministry trip. We were devastated. We had pooled all of our meager

---

35 Jeremiah 33:3
36 I Corinthians 14

resources to make this long journey of about sixty miles. We had fasted, prayed, and were full of expectation. Now what?

We may have been uncomplicated and naive by modern standards, but we were open on the "God-ward" side. When we returned to our mission we just dropped on our knees and cried out to the Lord. We first apologized for being so presumptuous, and then we pleaded for a divine visitation.

Suddenly the Spirit of the Lord came upon one of the young men and he began to prophecy, assuring us that we did not have to travel abroad (even across the river to Detroit or Toledo) to find the word of the Lord for us. The gift of prophecy was present in our midst and this was the beginning of the manifestations of spiritual gifts and revelations in our little group. I am so glad that God marvelously answered our petitions over the years. He prompted us to believe for His divine intervention, even in spite of our immaturity. I am convinced that the Lord is raising up a mighty band of youth in these days who will demonstrate God's grace and glory to this untoward generation.

"Your sons and your daughters shall prophecy." [37]

Often the Lord would send us gifted ministers, some from as far away as Holland. One was our dear Dutch brother John Spillenar, who in his broken English exhorted us to study the word. Many times we would kneel in our little chapel prayer room in God's overwhelming presence to be taught the living oracles of God. I especially remember studying Romans five. I suddenly realized that I was not under condemnation, but that I had been justified by faith. It was just as though I had never sinned. I was learning to reign in this life in Christ.

By that time we too had heard the sound of abundance of rain. Our quest for the spiritual gifts and for the conversion of souls was further stimulated by reading awesome reports of the healing revivals that were sweeping

---

[37] Joel 2:23-28

our nation. We were also receiving great reports from Dr. Charles Price and from various healing magazines like the *Voice of Healing* which was written by Gordon Lindsay. We were sold out to God and waiting eagerly for His divine outpouring. We believed that we were on the threshold of the restoration of all that the prophets have spoken about.[38] As we waited in the presence of the Lord we were blessed by wonderful seasons of refreshing.

The Sound of Abundance of Rain

We had entered a new season of revival and times of refreshing from the presence of the Lord. The glory clouds were laden with heavenly rain that was already falling around us as mercy drops, but we could "hear the sound of abundance of rain" [39]

At the same time God was already doing a mighty work in Detroit, Michigan, at the Bethesda Missionary Temple. News of the phenomenal outpouring of the Holy Spirit traveled fast. This was the time of the "Latter Rain!" Powerful new choruses were birthed, as well as prophetic songs of the Lord.

The founding pastor, M. D. "Mom" Beall was a mighty woman of God. She was raised in the Methodist tradition. She tells of kneeling by her gas stove with the oven door open to keep warm and praying fervently to receive the baptism of the Holy Spirit. The Lord met her in a glorious way and granted her desire. She was filled with the Holy Spirit and spoke in a heavenly language. Other people saw the great change in her countenance and life, and some asked her about how to receive this baptism in the Holy Ghost. Not yet a theologian, she would reply, "Well, you just open your oven door and kneel down, and God will fill you." During the early days of the new depression-era church, Pastor Beall was given a word from the Lord to build a

---

[38] Acts 3:18-21
[39] 1 Kings 18:41

tremendous 2500 seat "armory" adjacent to their basement church in Detroit.

Pastor Beall and her family had heard of the "Latter Rain" outpouring in Canada. The Bealls traveled to Vancouver, B.C., on the west coast of Canada where the "Latter Rain" group from North Battleford, Saskatchewan, had gone to conduct prophetic presbytery meetings at a camp. At that meeting the word of the Lord given to "Mom" Beall, through the prophetic presbytery, was a powerful confirmation of all that the Lord had spoken to her about the "armory" in Detroit. She returned to her congregation with the fresh touch of God on her life, and revival broke out spontaneously in their basement church. (The new sanctuary was almost completed at that time.)

The next Sunday, Pastor James Lee Beall, the eldest son of M. D. Beall, led the morning worship service in his customary manner. Suddenly, the whole congregation broke out in spontaneous worship with a new sound from heaven. It was the birthing of the song of the Lord. Many called it the "heavenly choir." After this phenomenal outpouring, a new and refreshing atmosphere of worship prevailed in every service. It was characterized by heavenly harmony. This became the hallmark of the revival which bore the title of "Latter Rain."

Those were epochal days for us also in our little mission in Windsor. We had heard the joyful sound.[40] Our whole passion and focus was to live and move in the flow of this very present truth.

Meanwhile, in Bethesda, we were caught up in a revival that was to go on seven days a week, day and night in the new "armory" for over three years. The large new sanctuary was packed every day. The reverberations of this mighty visitation were to be felt in almost every quarter of our nation and in many nations abroad. Many believers came from around the world who received spiritual impartations that were taken back to their homes and churches.

---

[40] Psalm 89:15

During this same time a large number of healing evangelists came to prominence in America. Among them was fifteen-year-old "Little David Walker" who preached in Bethesda Church every night for six weeks with mighty signs and wonders following. We attended great meetings with men like William Branham, F.F. Bosworth, Ernest Baxter, Oral Roberts, A.A. Allen, Jack Coe, W.V. Grant, T.L. Osborne and many others who were literally traversing the nations. We lived in a continual state of great expectation.

Chapter Five

Betty Lou

It was during these days of revival that the Lord arranged for my first encounter with a beautiful young member of Bethesda Missionary Temple. Betty Lou Teachout Winans arrived with her mother, stepfather Ralph Winans, and her two sisters. Ralph Winans had come to preach at our little mission on Parent Avenue in Windsor. Betty's mom sang many songs, especially, "Walking up the King's Highway," and had a great anointing on her. I was struck with Betty's beauty and sweet spirit, and we immediately both felt a deep bonding in the spirit. It was evident that we were destined to become lifelong friends. I stopped often in Detroit to see Betty who worked near the bus station in downtown Detroit. (I traveled primarily by bus to my meetings in those early days.)

The revival was on in Bethesda Church. There was a great host of denominational leaders of renown who came and were ministered to by the prophetic presbytery there. Among them were Stanley Frodsham, editor of the *Pentecostal Evangel*, and key leaders of major Pentecostal denominations. Men like Garland Pemberton, Charles Green, Thomas Wyatt, Erskine Holt, Elmer Frink, and John Poole participated in these meetings and left a rich deposit of God's Word.

At the same time we were also witnessing a great move of God in our little mission church on Parent Avenue in Windsor. My brother Bill was the pastor of the mission which consisted of mostly young believers. The presence of the Lord was so real that we often could smell the heavenly aroma of Jesus. People were set free from demons and diseases, and many families were reunited as the church grew rapidly.

Exercising the Call

During this time Bill would assign me to preach periodically in our home church. We also traveled together to several places in Ontario and the United States. All the while we kept preaching the simple Gospel and contending for all the gifts of the Spirit and we exercised the powerful prophetic mantle that the Lord had already laid upon us. We felt like were walking in The Acts of the Apostles. The very air was electric with expectation. During these years great stadiums and arenas across the land were being filled with people who were hungry for the Gospel and the manifest power of God. The Latter Rain was falling!

In 1948 Billy Graham launched a mighty tent revival in Los Angeles. This meeting became the launching place of his successive years of ministry around the world. Billy told us that he heard God challenge him to preach the simple Gospel and always to make a "bee-line" to the cross. It was there in Los Angeles that Randolph Hearst, the newspaper magnate, was touched by the Lord and he instructed all of his newspapers nationwide to "Puff Graham."

I had asked Betty to attend one of Billy's meetings on one of our first dates. The meeting was in the Coliseum in Detroit. She asked for time off from her job at the Kresge's five and dime store so she could attend Billy's meeting with me. Betty's boss said, "Sure, but don't bother coming back. You're fired." Billy is still alive as I write this (he just turned 94). What a great man of God and patriarch of the faith he is!

Great healing tents sprouted up like so many mushrooms across the landscape. City after city flashed the news of signs and wonders and miracles. Oral Roberts claimed that he laid hands on over 1.5 million people during his "Healing Waters" meetings. Many people in numerous cities testified to miraculous healings or deliverance from demons.

Oral Roberts pioneered television coverage of his meetings that brought him before multiplied millions all over the world. I had the pleasure of witnessing one of Brother

Roberts' first tent meetings in 1948 in Granite City, Illinois. I was preaching a revival in a Pentecostal church in the same city at the age of fifteen.

Oral and I became friends over the years, and I was invited at a very strategic time to share a word with the board of directors at Oral Roberts University. Later I was invited to spend time with Richard Roberts during his transition as the second president of ORU. We were honored to know Oral Roberts and to be with him in his home during his last days where he continued to minister to many who visited him there. We also shared fellowship with him at our home church, Life Church in Irvine, California, with Pastor Phil Munsey. Brother Roberts passed on to his reward in 2011. He was a remarkable man of God.

The Lord used many gifted and some unusual people in the spread of the "Latter Rain." Someone has said this "charismatic flame has attracted a lot of peculiar bugs." Many books have been written about portions of this season of visitation, and I am sure many more could be written. Suffice it to say that it was a time of divine intervention, and a powerful confirmation of the Word of the Lord that had been given to us in our early beginnings. My little raft kept progressing on the "stream of life" by the grace of God.

After the Rain

I was now experiencing a recurring vision and beginning to witness the fulfillment of that original prophetic word that the Lord had given to me in Toronto in the early part of 1947. New doors of ministry began to open to me. I would fast and pray and get a fresh word from the Lord. (I called it getting my gun loaded.) Then I would wait for the phone to ring. Invariably someone would call to invite me to come and minister in a church in one state or another.

I received a call to preach a revival meeting in Paducah, Kentucky. No one had told me it was hard to do, so I just obeyed and went. My Mom and Dad laid their hands on me and prayed over me, committing me to the Lord's keeping. I had no fear; just exhilarating joy. I remember packing my little suitcase and taking the bus through the Windsor-Detroit Tunnel and being quite nervous passing through the U.S. Customs and Immigration.

"Where are you going?"

"I am going to preach in Kentucky!"

"You are what?"

After more interrogation, the officer just shook his head and said, "Go on." Then I boarded an old Greyhound bus at the Detroit Bus Station with a one-way ticket.

We were soon on our way heading out for Paducah through many secondary roads. (There were no interstate highways in those days.) The bus broke down only once on that trip, and we finally arrived after about fourteen hours. The Pentecostal Church was located at Fifth and Jackson Street. The pastors were Brother and Sister Mills. God met us in a marvelous way with His favor, and many precious souls were added to His Kingdom. This meeting opened up many new doors in the "free" Pentecostal churches in several states.

One of the great highlights of my life was when Pastor Guy Walsh of Benton Harbor, Michigan invited me to preach at the Benton Harbor Tabernacle. Brother Walsh was one of the great preachers of my day, and he led a very large congregation. While there I spent some delightful hours in his wonderful library. He became a tremendous example to me of a man who studied and prayed at least eight hours a day. Pastor Walsh trusted me to preach at his great church. He even trusted me to pastor his church while he went abroad to Israel for six weeks. I was all of fifteen years old, and I am forever indebted to men like Brother Walsh who believed in me, mentored me, and encouraged me on my journey. My sweetheart Betty drove over with some friends from Detroit to visit me there. It was an exciting time in the Lord.

I kept traveling for several months as the Lord opened new doors of ministry for me: from Kentucky to Indiana, Tennessee, and Michigan, then back to Ontario to the Indian reservations. I felt right at home ministering among the

Indians again at Oshweken, Ontario, and the Six Nations Reserve. I lived for a season at 14 Sanderson Street, in Brantford, Ontario, with Mom and Pa Miller and their five children. Out of this divine connection the Lord touched the heart of Dan Miller, their son, to join me in ministry in Huntingburg, Indiana. After preaching in that town we felt constrained to venture together into new territories, and preach the Gospel in several other places.

Moses and Daniel at Cup Creek Church

Moses and Daniel

The Lord led us to a little Baptist Church near Velpen, Indiana, that was called "Cup Creek Community Baptist Church." It was visited every three weeks by their circuit riding pastor. God gave us favor with the presiding deaconess, and we were granted the privilege of preaching each night there for three weeks in between the pastor's visits. The old building was run down. The doors were hanging loose on broken hinges, overlapping and held shut by a big rock. We rolled back the rock, swept the house, and lit the pot-belly stove in the middle of the room. Revival was on!

While in that area Dan and I were asked to stay with George and Sybil Hollenberg who had a spacious farm house. Sybil was the presiding deaconess. She was also a wonderful cook and a "mom" to us during our time there. George was not yet a believer, but he received us kindly. He was one of our early converts in a revival that moved a large portion of that community.

People who had been converted in our revival were coming in to the local general store and paying their old debts. Kenny Houchins, the store-keeper, thanked us for so many miraculous payments. One man who was converted during the revival brought back an old Ford truck with a plow on it. He had borrowed the plow from Kenny years before and never had returned it. He now felt like the truck should be given as interest for the years he had failed to return the plow. This was a sign of true revival that affected the whole area.

We kept plowing through slush, snow and mud each night for about ten weeks. The Melvin Houchin's family let us drive their new '49 Ford station wagon. We loaded it up with people we picked up along the way. It was amazing to see what the Lord did with two young lads from Canada who were totally dependent on the Holy Spirit. Dan played his guitar, and I played the accordion as we sang duets together. We sowed the seed of the Gospel in weakness, and God raised it in power.

One Sunday we baptized thirty-two new converts in the nearly frozen Cup Creek. Our host, George, was reluctant to be baptized because he thought it was too cold. He thought it would be better to be baptized in the horse trough in his barn since he had a serious arthritic condition. We persuaded him that he too was to publicly identify with Jesus in His burial and His resurrection. He was the first to plunge into the frozen waters of baptism and he came out healed!

Later during the meetings God sent us Pastor John Deering, a good man who helped us build a new church building on land donated by one of our converts. This intensely dedicated group all pitched in and built a lovely little church that still stands as a testimony to God's abiding grace. We were able to see two new churches planted that spring: one in Cup Creek, near Velpen, Indiana, and the other church in nearby Robinson, Illinois.

Back to Windsor

We were physically exhausted after our meetings, so we returned home to Windsor for a time of rest, recovery, and refreshing. The Lord had put it on my heart to check on the "Convention Hall" property. It was owned by a local church that was led by our friends and located on Lake Erie near Wheatley, Ontario. I was at that point seventeen years old. Dan and I drove out to see Pastor Enoch Nelson at the Coatsworh, Ontario, Pentecostal Church. Brother Enoch agreed to lease us the great hall (fifty-four bedrooms, plus a dining hall and an auditorium) for $1,000 for the entire summer with no down payment. This marvelous Tudor type building was built by the Detroit Police Club during the prohibition days in the U.S.A. They claimed bankruptcy when the prohibition ceased, and it was sold, unfinished, to the Coatsworth Church.

Convention Hall, Lakeside, Wheatley, Ont., Canada.

We were so excited with the prospect of starting this camp. No one had told me it was hard to do. So Dan Miller and I gathered a group of family friends (including my dear friend, Betty) and we started cleaning the massive place. We swept out spiders, set up beds, repaired plumbing, and brought in groceries. God gave us His favor with the local grocer and butcher who allowed us to charge all our food until after the camp was over. The Lord sent us many workers who helped us launch the "Fair Haven Camp." Our friends, Mom and Pop Miller, were wonderful helpers in so many ways, especially as cooks. We were able to purchase this place later for only five thousand dollars. It was located on five acres of land. Quite a few ministries were launched from that camp. To God be the glory! Then, on December 6, 1961, the camp burned down due to faulty wiring.

There were times when my little raft hit some turbulent waters. Sometimes the word of the Lord tried us, just as it did Joseph.[41] At times the vision would tarry, but we had to wait for it. It would surely come to pass and not be a day late. That was my experience in those exciting days when we walked under God's divine oversight, even when the stream I was traveling on my little raft brought me through places of severe turbulence. At that time there was never a day that I did not feel His mighty Holy Spirit upon me, and I constantly prayed in the Spirit.

It was about 1950 when the Lord provided me with my first car, a beautiful 1940 Ford Deluxe Sedan. (I wish I had it now.) I borrowed $400 from my dad to purchase it. We called her "Shasta." She hasta to have gas, she hasta have oil, she hasta have tires. She also carried us to many places because she hasta get us there and back.

Dan and I launched out in that Ford to many new destinations. We were preaching the good news and seeing many souls saved and filled with the Spirit. It seemed that there were many young people being called into ministry in those days. I am amazed at the great doors that the Lord opened for us. I would be remiss if I didn't tell you what I feel the Lord impressing deep within me now.

"For God's gifts and His call are irrevocable. He never withdraws them once they are given, and He does not change His mind about those to whom He gives His grace or to whom He sends His call." [42]

---

[41] Psalm 105:19
[42] Romans 11:29 TAB

I believe I am speaking to you as you read this "chronicle." God has never been sorry that He called you. I challenge you to stir up your gift and report for duty. Let me tell you more about the awesome preparations and equipping that the Lord allowed me to go through. God seldom calls the qualified,[43] but He does qualify those whom He has called.

Seasons of Refreshing Evangelism

As I traveled in ministry I was surrounded by many young ministers, even teen-agers, who emerged with little fanfare and yet they radiated a great zeal for God. These young evangelists didn't hold conferences on faith healing. They merely read the red, prayed for the power, and healed the sick. I witnessed this in many parts of our nation and in other nations as well. This kind of true faith and spiritual power is especially evident today in communist China.

I have had the privilege of living through several major visitations of the Holy Spirit, but I sincerely believe that we are now on the verge of yet another season of divine intervention. Malachi 3:1 opens to us the scenario of our Lord Jesus coming "to His church" before he comes "for His church." This was to be more than a one night stand; more than a visitation. He was coming to inhabit by sitting (a judicial stance) and purifying the sons of Levi, His New Testament priests. That's you and me. We are destined to have the sanctifying power of His Holy Spirit flame purge us as priestly sons of Levi so that we may offer to the Lord an offering in righteousness.

Many preachers read from Malachi three and rush to verse ten that speaks about bringing all of the tithe into His storehouse. That is a vital and legitimate part of His habitation, but I believe that judgment has already begun in the house of the Lord. The refiner's fire is beginning to single out ministries that have deviated from the course of true holiness.

---

[43] I Corinthians 1:26-31

All the World's a Stage

While traveling with the Lord on my "little raft" on the streams of inspiration the Lord revealed to me in a vision the great stage of life. Shakespeare wrote, "'All the world's a stage." Man lives through seven stages. The Lord showed me that many who are on the stage today are not playing according to the Script(ures). He then showed me that He was removing many of the "star" characters and players who had deviated from the script. He is replacing the cast for the last act, and the people He uses are going to stay with the script that is contained in the simple Gospel. We are going to see a mighty display of signs, wonders, and miracles. The Lord will revive His work in the midst of the years. A people who "do know their God shall do exploits."[44] Jesus is walking among His golden lampstands.[45] His piercing eyes see our desperate shortcomings, and yet He calls us to return in repentance and do our first works over again. He has said, "I will build My church, and the gates of hell shall not prevail against it!" [46]

---

[44] Daniel 11:32
[45] Revelation 2:1
[46] Mathew 16:18-19

Chapter Six

The Power of

Reciprocation

My induction into the Lord's Levitical training process has caused me to experience the powerful fulfillment of my prophetic calling and my function as a New Testament priest. I was learning to be a "bearer of His presence" as I traveled out of my comfort zone at home. I was now thrust on the ever expanding stream of revelation as I continued training for the reigning. My "little raft" was moving rapidly on the tide of spontaneous revelation. These were seasons of refreshing from the presence of the Lord. I was learning that it was *"good for a man to bear the yoke in his youth"*[47] and to carry the mantle of ministry and to fulfill the highest call of all. It was also my desire to be associated with more mature young people as well as with seasoned ministers. Many gifted men helped to mentor me and compelled me to take big steps in faith.

I learned that we may have *"ten thousand instructors, but not many fathers."*[48] My delight was, and still is, to meet with mature men and women of God who encouraged, motivated, and taught me the power of reciprocation in ministry. The art of "sharpening axes"[49] became my aspiration. I also was instructed by the Lord in ways to "gauge" a person's depth[50] and to learn to "draw out waters of wisdom and knowledge." Progressive revelation is still my quest.

The Lord continued confirming His word with marvelous signs, wonders, and with precious souls being spiritually transformed and filled with the Holy Spirit. We also modeled the template of every believer becoming a witness. I tried to encourage new believers to pursue their calls. In the early

---

[47] Lamentations 3:27
[48] I Corinthians 4:15
[49] Proverbs 27:17
[50] Proverbs 20:5

days of our little group of about one hundred young people in Windsor, Ontario, almost everyone knew what his calling was and how to make it sure.[51] It was a blessing to be able to encourage many young folks to answer the call to full-time ministry, and we are so grateful for those still active today.

Developing a Hearing Ear

When I was about seventeen years old and ministering in Robinson, Illinois, the Lord met me in a very special way. Early each morning I was directed to read Isaiah chapter fifty. Here I discovered in verses four and five the Messianic prophecy relating to Jesus.

"The Lord God has given me the tongue of the learned [disciplined one] that I should know how to speak a word in season to him that is weary. He awakens me morning by morning, He awakens my ear to hear as the learned. The Lord God has opened my ear; and I was not rebellious, nor did I turn away."

This became my prayer and my lifelong goal. I made a covenant with the Lord that I would not leave my room in the morning until He awakened me and opened my ears to hear. I determined that I would follow on to know His voice as He instructed me to. I also began to see that Jesus was never need oriented, nor need controlled. He was command-oriented and thus He was command-controlled. He encouraged me to be the same way!

For example, he demonstrated this so powerfully in his first miracle at a wedding in Cana of Galilee.[52] His mother informed him of an embarrassing situation: the governor of the wedding feast had announced that they had run out of wine. Jesus said to her, *"Woman, what does your concern have to do with me? My hour has not yet come."* Mary knew that He would hear from the Father, so she told the servants, *"Whatever he says to you, do it!"*

---

[51] II Peter 1:10
[52] John 2:1-11

Jesus did hear from His Father, and the rest of the incident is well-known. He transformed over one hundred and twenty gallons of water into excellent wine, and, I believe, confirmed the sanctity of marriage with His miraculous provision. This beginning of signs Jesus did in Cana of Galilee. He manifested His glory, and His disciples believed in Him. I have learned over the years that Jesus has us tied to Himself by His voice. (My umbilical cord is His voice.) In John ten, Jesus said, *"My sheep know My voice, and a stranger they will not follow."* Jesus never said anything except what He heard His Father tell Him. The Father told Him what to say and how to say it. [53]

God is Not Giving You the Silent Treatment

Our God speaks and we are wired for sound. He says, *"Call on Me and I will answer you, and I will show you great and mighty things that you have never known."* [54] God always says something before He does something. In the beginning was the Word, the Word was God manifest in the flesh. In your every new beginning there must be a Word.

"The Lord God will not do anything until he reveals His secrets to His servants the prophets." [55]

This is God's method of operation. He says:

The things unto the those that be belong unto us and to our children and our children's children, forevermore. [56]

> The voice of the Lord is continuous. Only our hearing is intermittent.

secret belong Lord, but things revealed

---

[53] John 12:49
[54] Jeremiah 33:3
[55] Amos 3:7
[56] Deuteronomy 29:29

God still speaks to those who have ears to hear. Eight times in the Revelation of Jesus Christ, we read *"He that has ears to hear let him hear what the Spirit is saying to the churches."* Are your ears awake? Many quote God, but few sound like Him.

Jesus Promises Another Comforter

"However, I am telling you nothing but the truth when I say it is profitable (good, expedient, advantageous) for you that I go away; because if I go not away, the Comforter (Counselor, Helper, Advocate, Intercessor, Strengthener, Standby) will not come to you [into close fellowship with you]; but if I go away, I will send Him to you [to be in close fellowship with you]." [57]

How I praise God for His Comforter. In my journey with Jesus I learned to respond to His voice. I resolved that I would be "voice activated." If I listened and obeyed, I found that the results were amazing. Obedience is the key. It is better than sacrifice. I discovered that revelation truth must move me to right action, or that same truth would move me to self-deception.[58] The Holy Spirit was given to lead us and guide us into all truth. I didn't have to move on my own whims. I did not have to create an agenda. I was constantly made aware that He would guide me with His eye, and that I could hear His voice behind me saying, *"This is the way, walk in it."*[59] It always begins in the morning when He awakens me, and I pray it will be your daily experience as well.

---

[57] John 16:7 Amplified Bible
[58] James 1:22
[59] Isaiah 30:21

God's Word Endures Forever

God's word that goes forth from His mouth will never return void. God watches over His word to perform it. This awesome word has sustained many, including Bible heroes like Joseph, Jeremiah, and many of those in the roll call of the faithful recorded in Hebrews chapter eleven. God's Word sustains me too as I press on in my journey with Him. The vision He gave me as a lad was forever imprinted in my heart and mind. It has never left me and is renewed daily as I wait at His gate. Morning by morning He awakens me to a new adventure. "Where are we going today, Jesus?"

On one occasion, I was preparing to go ice-skating with a youth group in Brantford, Ontario. The Lord gently spoke to me and said, *"If you will stay I will reveal Myself to you."* I was really intent on going, but I said, "Yes Lord." As I heard the laughter of the other teenagers fading away into the night I fell on my knees by my bed. I was somewhat torn emotionally as I opened the Word to Psalm 32. Here the Lord confirmed His covenant with me, that He would guide me with His eye. I was not be like a horse that needs a bit and bridle to jerk it around as he rushes into battle, nor like a mule that needs prodding to get it moving. God wanted my neck reigned with His gentle nudges. He was turning me in the way He wanted me to go."[60] This was a definite turning point in my life. I am so glad that I stayed home that night!

Learning to be "voice-activated" is a lifelong pursuit. You will become less agitated about circumstances, less anxious about your future, and totally dependent on His voice. I like to call this mode "the sanctified I-don't-cares." I also discovered early on my journey that whatever way the Lord moved me, it was a promotion. *"Promotion comes from the Lord."[61]* The most good we do is inadvertent! Also, if you are a Christian, the worst things you do are done inadvertently.

---

[60] Psalm 32:8-10
[61] Psalm 75:6

The Lord would often pull my little raft to shore for a rest and He would recharge me. I would especially encourage my young followers to enter into this kind of rest with the Lord. "Rest-oration" (speaking out of rest) is God's ideal for you. The Lord taught me to preach by inspiration rather than by perspiration. You will discover that many folks will not understand you or appreciate the path you choose, but He invites you to come and follow Him in Holy abandonment.

Robert Frost said it well: "Two roads diverged in a wood, and I, I took the one less traveled by, and that has made all the difference." It was the path that *the vulture's eyes has not seen.*[62] Jesus called it the straight and narrow way, found by relatively very few.[63] Have you found that path? Would you ask Jesus to show you His ways today?

I like Eugene Peterson's translation of Mathew 11:28-30.

"Are you tired? Worn out? Burned out on religion? Come to me. Get away with me and you'll recover your life. I'll show you how to take a real rest. Walk with me and work with me---watch how I do it. Learn the unforced rhythms of grace. I won't lay anything heavy or ill-fitting on you. Keep company with me and you'll learn to live freely and lightly."

It has been said that some preachers need a travel agent to handle all the guilt trips they put on God's people. Jesus came not to condemn, but to seek and to save those who are lost.

There were times when Betty and I scraped the bottom of the barrel, but the Lord always heard when we scraped. I had developed a motto. Always give without imposing your gift, and always receive without expecting any more. This conviction of my heart was tested many times, but money was never a criterion for me in answering the call. In fact, right after my heavenly vision and calling in Toronto as a thirteen year old lad, I actually packed my little Samsonite suitcase with a few unmentionables and slid it under my

---

[62] Job 28:7
[63] Matthew 7:13-14

bed. I prayed each night for the Lord to send me a ticket to India, or anywhere, and I would be ready to go. I never thought about preparation or a return ticket. Just get me there! I believe I can honestly say I had childlike faith.

As a youth I decided to follow Jesus, with no turning back. Jesus said to me, "Follow me and I will make you." I have lived in anticipation of future grace. My goal was set: to go to all the nations of the earth to make disciples and to preach the Gospel of the unshakeable Kingdom of God.

At that time I was particularly drawn in my vision to the area then called East Bengal (later East Pakistan). It is now known as Bangladesh. I knew I would go there someday, but I knew I was to be faithful and bloom wherever God had planted me. In the meantime I was preparing my heart daily with fresh manna and feeding my vision. Don't let anyone steal your vision.

Chapter Seven

The Love of My Life

I had already met Betty, my sweetheart and future wife. She would often come over with her family to our mission in Windsor from Detroit, and we were definitely falling in love. Betty's Mom was an anointed singer and a saint. She had a vibrant spirit and was a great encouragement to us all. We suffered a great loss when the Lord took her to heaven at the very young age of forty. Betty was just fifteen years old at the time, so I never had a living mother-in-law. I had met her, and in my heart I believed she really liked me. She surely knows in heaven all about her family now.

Periodically I would return home to Windsor between meetings to be recharged, and sometimes I would work at a secular job just to keep preaching. Those were special days when I was just fifteen years old. My job was driving a loaded semi-trailer truck to the Chrysler plant in Detroit from Windsor. I would occasionally manage to swing by very early in the morning and wake Betty, to take her in my huge truck to the office at the gas company in downtown Detroit. (She often had to wait for her office to open at 8:00.) We had some delightful times just waiting together.

In my heart I knew that Betty was the one God had for me and would be with me forever. In my own naive way I would torment her with heavy questions about her willingness to travel with me even to primitive places like India; to live in a grass hut, to eat snakes and snails and puppy dog tails! Betty was always gentle and compliant. "Yes," she said. "I will go with you anywhere the Lord leads us," and she has. My love for Betty was and is deep and unshakeable. She is my very best friend to this day.

One of our first dates away from home was a trip we made to Findlay, Ohio, in 1948. Our good friends Wayne and Maxine Owens from Kentucky were preaching there. Seven of us piled into Dad's '42 De Soto in Windsor and we traveled to Findlay. It was about a three hour drive. Later we would see the hand of the Lord in that trip, as it introduced us to the church that would open to us to pastor ten years later. God was confirming His mighty plan and purpose in our lives.

In April, 1953, we were on a date on the old Detroit to Bob-Lo boat excursion. Red Harper (Shirley Boone's father) was the singing star on this Gospel music cruise. It was full of people enjoying a great Gospel concert and cruising on the Detroit River. Betty and I climbed up to the top deck which was quite deserted, and it was in this warm and wonderful moment that I proposed to her. Hallelujah, she accepted!

A few months later we were married in Windsor on August 29, 1953. Pastor William Fitch presided. The service was in the Bethel Assembly of God Church at the corner of Bruce and London Streets. It was sweltering weather, over 100 degrees, and they had no air-conditioning. We didn't even light the candles because they had already melted with the heat and fallen over. Our reception was upstairs in the old Smith auditorium where several hundred came to celebrate our wedding

Betty and Moses
August 29, 1953

reception. Mom and Pop Miller, our dear friends, blessed us again and helped prepare a massive chicken dinner which we all enjoyed immensely.

On our two week long honeymoon we traveled south to Florida in the '48 Chevrolet coupe that Betty's dad had given us as a wedding gift. We didn't have a care in the world and we just knew that the Lord had provided us with everything we needed. I remember that our entire gasoline expense was just $56. There were very few motels in those days. The ones we encountered were not very elaborate, but we made it.

Those bologna sandwiches and twenty-five cent large bottles of soda pop really tasted good.

We returned to our first home in Windsor, a home fully furnished for forty dollars a month rent, just a few doors down from the Gospel Tabernacle where we were pastoring. Betty had a good office job at the gas company in Detroit, and it really helped augment the $18 per week offerings that I averaged from our church in Windsor. Those were good days.

A Powerful Vision

It was here in our humble living room one night, as I was praying, that I saw in a beautiful vision a picture of my family to be. It's amazing, as I see that same picture on my office wall now. I saw Betty surrounded by six children. I was so naive at that time. I ran to her bedroom and told her about my "great revelation." She was not really impressed, as she was in the "ice cream and pickles" season of her first pregnancy. "You want five more? Dear Lord help us!" Well, the Lord did help us, and we eventually had six wonderful arrows in our quiver. Betty has been an awesome mom, wife, and faithful friend.

The Heritage of the Lord

Arrow Number One

Our first baby, Debbie Sue, was born July 5th, 1954. We were so thrilled with this very tiny little bundle of joy. We had become a real family! Debbie has had several physical handicaps in her life but has maintained a beautiful spirit through it all. Her husband, Bob Olmstead, was part of our Findlay church as a young boy. He has been a loving caregiver to Debbie, and they faithfully serve the Lord together. Debbie and Bob have three great children: Jonathan, Jeremy, and Jessica, who have all served in the military. Today they also have three beautiful granddaughters.

In March of 2002 Debbie was very sick with a strange and severe illness called "vasculitus" that came upon her suddenly. She was treated at local hospitals and later spent several weeks in the Cleveland Clinic. She was paralyzed, blind, and deaf. Our sweet girl languished in the intensive care unit with no hope of recovery. Suddenly one morning, as we stood around her bed, Jesus came to her in the ICU ward. She cried out, "Hey! Don't you know that Jesus Christ is my Savior? Don't you know that Jesus is my healer? And don't you know that I am a minister's daughter?" Debbie had never acted or expressed herself that way before. Then she continued. "Satan, get out of here!" She then lifted her paralyzed hand and swung it in a powerful motion. The bells and signals on the monitors went wild. Doctors and nurses ran in, and Debbie was set free! She could raise her hands, her feet, and she said, "Doctor, I see your tie and it is yellow; and oh, yes, there is "Tweetie Bird." (It was an inflated get well balloon by her bed.) Debbie and Bob live near us now in California and we see a miracle every time we meet. She is a great source of joy to us all.

Arrow Number Two

Our son, Thomas Dale, was born in Middlesboro, Kentucky, on January 29, 1957. He was our largest baby, weighing almost ten pounds. Tom was a fine little boy who brought us comfort and joy as we pastored in this quaint little town in the hills of Kentucky.

As Tom matured he was very sensitive to people and spiritual things. Tom was very much engaged in our church building programs and to this day says he learned much for his future careers from working at Hope Temple. He was also gifted in music and drama, and he became a great help to me in many areas of church administration. Tom earned excellent grades in school and in college.

One day when he was about twenty years old he shocked us all by volunteering to join the Marine Corps. As our first child left the nest we were nearly traumatized. Later on we became so proud of what the Marine Corps accomplished in training Tom. He became a respected marine officer and top notch jet pilot! All along the Lord's hand of grace was on

Tom's life. In March of 1980 we were honored to perform the wedding as Tom married Maria Bingham while he was stationed in Kingsville, Texas.

They were soon blessed with two precious and active boys whom they named Caleb and Joshua. When Joshua was about fifteen months old he wandered out to their back yard swimming pool and drowned. Our hearts were broken. We pleaded for and received the Lord's comfort, grace and mercy.

A little over a year later Maria delivered another beautiful baby boy. Dustin weighed over ten pounds at birth, but they discovered that he had not developed properly internally. His precious little soul went on to heaven just a few minutes after he was born. Needless to say the trauma of these successive losses was almost unbearable for Tom, Maria, and all the family. This tremendous loss prompted Tom to resign from the Marine Corps. His heart was broken, and he had an overwhelming desire to be with his little family. Only the Lord knows the depths of grief that inundated Tom and Maria, but through these sorrowful experiences God instilled a great depth of character and compassion in both of their hearts.

Later the Lord graciously blessed Tom and Maria with two more precious boys, Thomas West and Austin David. They have grown into fine young men who love the Lord and are progressing in their quest for God's divine purpose in their lives. To Tom and Maria's great delight their last child was a girl. Autumn Marie was the final arrow in their quiver. Today she is a beautiful, talented, and dedicated follower of Jesus. She has a heart to serve others and will doubtless be used mightily by the Lord. Autumn is Tom and Maria's princess. We are so proud of them all!

After Tom resigned from the Marine Corp he launched into a successful MBA degree program from USC Irvine. He then went on to receive his executive MBA from Harvard University. The Lord opened the way some time later for Tom to become the president and owner of Maranatha! Music Company. He built the company into a very successful

Christian business and sold it in 2005. He is presently an executive working in design and development for a large construction company. We are so grateful for his generosity and his gifts of help to us, as well as to other worthy Christian ministries.

A Brand New Creation

Tom and Maria's oldest son Caleb Moses, who as a boy was a California surfer, became addicted to heavy drugs. After long years of intercession by many family members he was totally delivered from drug addiction. Caleb had a powerful spiritual transformation early in 2011. He has since completed training at Teen Challenge, and WYWAM in Kona, Hawaii. Caleb called me one day and said, "Grandpa, I am a brand new creation. I am not a recovering anything." Since then Caleb has been successfully preaching the gospel and leading missionary teams this past year to India, Krygistan, and Indonesia. As the Lord leads, Caleb will be joining me in mission trips this coming year. [64]

Arrow Number Three

Our third child, Becky Lou, was born in Windsor, Ontario, on January 17, 1958. Becky is an effervescent source of joy and continues to be a great blessing to us. Becky is gifted with a servant's heart. From her youth she has been like an associate mother to her siblings. Even as a child her devotion for her Lord was beautifully evident in everything she did.

Becky, as a young girl, loved to worship and was active in our church choir, in many drama presentations, and even in nursery duty. She literally radiated the joy of the Lord, and she became my receptionist at Hope Temple. She was always Mom's helper and was very sensitive to our needs. She has displayed her mother's talents in interior design and they both love to help others when asked. It's fun for them. Becky married her high school boyfriend Gail Sterling, a

---

[64] His web-site address is www.calebvegh.com

sports fan who later coached our Hope Temple Academy basketball team to a state championship. Gail and Becky served as our youth pastors for a number of years and are still active in ministry in Bradenton, Florida.

They have three beautiful children. Christian is a successful owner of Christian Sterling Jewelers in Perrysburg, Ohio, where he lives with his wife Rachel, a dedicated school teacher, and their precious daughter, Gracie. Next is Stephen Michael, an aspiring student in the University of Arizona and a gifted writer. Their beautiful daughter, Ashley graduated from Ohio State University and is married to Collin Balester, a major-league baseball pitcher who is now signed with the Texas Rangers. They have a darling daughter, Roslyn.

Arrow Number Four

Marcus Stephen was born December 14, 1959. He was promoted to heaven on October 20th, 2007. I will have much more to say about our beloved son, Marcus, later.

Arrow Number Five

Cathy Jan was born when our oldest child, Debbie, was just seven and a half years old. She was such a beautiful and compliant baby. Cathy has always been very artistic, talented, and dramatic. She entertained us from a very early age, often using her little brother Michael as her prop. Cathy finished high school in our Hope Temple Academy where she further developed her talents in music and art. She attended Oral Roberts University and received a full scholarship. She was also chosen to play violin on the nationally broadcast television orchestra team which was prominent at that time. Later, Cathy traveled to Europe with a worship team we sent from Hope Temple. The team helped found the Living Word Church in Aalsmeer, Holland, which is still a thriving, growing congregation.

Cathy married Randy Alward from southern California. He was an emerging young preacher who had received his training at Portland Bible College. I married them in Hope

Temple in 1983. They now have three handsome sons: Derek, Jordan and Chase. These young men have a real call of God on their lives, and they have each attended Portland Bible College. Randy is now the owner and president of Maranatha! Music Company. We really thought that Cathy Jan was our caboose, but four and a half years later another blessing came to Moses and Betty.

Arrow Number Six

Michael Todd was born October 7, 1966. He was surrounded by loving siblings that were ready and able to babysit, and that helped make our "Mikey" a great delight. Michael has always been brilliant, and his mom would say he was the last child who inherited all her brains! Michael is a humble, tender-hearted, gentle, loving son. He was a voracious reader, and can to this very day converse on almost any subject you might mention.

Michael as a youth was a very good scholar, and he also graduated from our Hope Temple Christian Academy. Michael had a real heart for God and was involved with the work of the ministry as a skilled musician. He was proficient playing the cello, keyboards, the guitar, and the bass. He loved helping on the new sanctuary building as part of the crew, fearlessly climbing the highest rafters and scaring us all, while encouraging the builders. Michael graduated from Christ for the Nations Bible College when he was about twenty years old with a real passion to help expand the Kingdom of God. We have great expectations knowing that the hand of the Lord is upon Michael for good. Michael is employed as a very capable web-site designer, living nearby.

My Proverbs Thirty-One Lady

My wife Betty is the inspiration of my heart and life. As a young pastor I was extremely busy. I look back now with sincere regret that I did not give her more of my undivided attention. I know now that God wanted me to put my dear wife before others and any other work, no matter how spiritual it seemed. I have asked her and the Lord for forgiveness and have made every effort to make it up to her.

Over the years, Betty was totally given to her ministry of helps and hospitality. In addition to caring lovingly for our six children she was always ready to entertain company or facilitate activities related to the church. She is my Proverbs 31 woman. We are now completing sixty years of marriage, and once again I say with all my heart, "Betty, you are wonderful! You are my first and only girlfriend, and you are still my best friend. I love you with all my heart."

Launching Out Together

In 1954 while I was traveling in Illinois I was asked to be the pastor of the Bethel Pentecostal Church in East Alton. We were excited as we arrived there in April of 1954 where I celebrated my twenty-first birthday. I was also a new immigrant to the United States. Our first child, Debbie Sue, was born there. God gave us a great family of friends, many of whom are friends to this day. This was a real "stretching time" of learning to grow in grace and pastoral experience and we enjoyed our time there. We were so happy with our little four room parsonage built onto the rear of the church.

After about a year we resigned our pastorate and traveled back up to Canada to conduct our summer camp at Convention Hall in Wheatley, Ontario. We lived for a few months in the convention hall with our baby daughter, Debbie. It was quite a large home for the three of us: just fifty-four bedrooms.

Adventures in Kentucky

Later that fall we were invited to minister in Middlesboro, Kentucky. The leadership team asked me to become the pastor of the Avondale Avenue Pentecostal Church. We settled into our little parsonage in a "holler" with one mountain behind us and another before us. I remember a very special little bird who woke me morning by morning saying, "Preacher, preacher, preacher." (At least, I thought that is what he said.) That was a very special time of getting into the word every morning. I am still drawing from the reservoir of study in God's word that became so real to me in those Kentucky days. We had a phone, but we hardly ever heard it ring. Our income averaged about forty dollars per week, along with all the green beans and sow belly that we could eat. We dearly loved our church family there and it was a great training season for us.

Our first son, Tom, was born there in Middlesboro. Shortly after his birth we resigned our church and headed out in our 28-foot Miracle Marlette house-trailer, towed by our '54 De Soto. We traveled to evangelistic meetings with our two sweet children, Debbie and Tom.

Moses and Betty with Jim and Ann Beall, 2003

Chapter Eight   *A Door of Hope*

After traveling in our trailer home for a short time we sold it to help keep food on the table. We landed in Windsor, Ontario, again where we were provided an apartment by my parents. Those were severely trying days for our little family. Every door that seemed open to us closed. We were really in the dark room being processed by the Holy Spirit. The Word of the Lord tried me daily. Although we prayed fervently, we also kept on "eating" our furniture each week as we would sell off something just to keep living.

Becky Lou was born during that time. What a great blessing she was (and still is). After several months of just getting by and not telling anyone about our financial needs we were coming into the Christmas season. We were literally scraping the bottom of the barrel. I had actually cut down the cherry tree (like George Washington) by our little apartment just to have fuel for our stove. I had borrowed $100 from the bank so we could have a bit of Christmas for the kids. How long, Lord? We refused to tell anyone of our plight. It was really strange, but even our immediate family thought we were doing just fine.

One morning as I arose early the Lord "opened my ear to hear." I heard the Lord speak clearly. "I will turn your captivity today." I met Betty in our little kitchen and said, "Honey, God spoke to me and said that He would turn our captivity today."

"Oh yeah," she said, as she was plainly unmoved. She then asked me to go to the store and buy a few things. It was bitterly cold in Windsor, and it was snowing with slush and rain. I drove in my old De Soto down to the corner store.

It was our custom to listen to Pastor James Beall from Detroit each morning on his "America to Your Knees" broadcast. I switched on the radio and of course I knew the format. Every day there was an introduction, followed by a song by the trio, and then Pastor Jim would say, "Now let's turn to the Bible text…"

But that broadcast was different. Jim was ready to open his text when he stopped and said clearly, "O Man of God, you heard God speak to you this morning saying He was turning your captivity. Now believe it!" Wow! I began to cry. I could hardly see the road for my tears. I rushed back home and I met Betty at the door. Her countenance was bright. "Did you hear Brother Jim?" she cried. "Do you believe he was speaking to us?" Of course I did, and yes, he was speaking to us.

That very day we received a call from our dear friend, Rev. A.W. Thomas, Assistant General Superintendent of the Pentecostal Church of God. He asked us to go to Findlay, Ohio, to try out for the pastorate of the Blanchard Avenue Pentecostal Church of God. We arrived in Findlay to candidate and we were voted in by the forty-two members ·present. What a great day!

Our Captivity was Turned

It was time for our little raft to get moving. We soon packed our meager belongings that we had left in Windsor, Ontario, into a 4' by 8' trailer (It was nearly half full) and headed for our promised land in Findlay, Ohio. That was a very epochal moment for us. We had exhausted all our funds. In fact, we blew a tire on our way down at Bowling Green, Ohio, just fifteen miles north of Findlay. Providentially the tire died of natural causes right in front of a Goodyear tire shop. We prayed for favor and the kind repairman who helped us said, "Your tire is shot, and you have no spare. I have a used tire that should get you into Findlay." I asked him to give me a price. He replied, "I will change and replace your blown tire for two dollars." He had no way of knowing that we had exactly two dollars between us.

Some of the members of the Findlay church were waiting for us as we pulled up in front of our new parsonage. They had brought several packages of groceries to fill our cupboards. We thought we had died and gone to heaven. We celebrated that Christmas in Findlay, and every day thereafter seemed like Christmas to us. The people of Findlay will forever be near and dear to our hearts. Betty was and continues to be a skilled and compassionate homemaker, and she made us all very comfortable. We were home at last. A great sense of destiny and fulfillment prevailed in my heart. We were on the threshold of great opportunities in God.

The Lord had brought us to a place of rest and exciting expectations on our journey. We were now exploring our promised land. I would liken our Findlay ministry to our "book of Numbers" experience. The Lord God gave us a great congregation that was willing to go in and posses the land by building two new sanctuaries. While serving there the Lord also enabled me to travel extensively to the nations. I shall forever be grateful for this wonderful family of Hope that received us, loved us, and supported us faithfully and abundantly for twenty-seven years.

I was a young pastor with a gracious wife and three children when we were initiated into the Pentecostal Church of God. Betty and I recalled our first date, ten years earlier, which was our first trip to this church in Findlay. We felt that God had especially prepared us for that place and that we would be there for a very long time. In fact, on our honeymoon we stopped to see old Uncle Billie, a mountaineer living in southern Indiana. He told us that he had a vision of

The Vegh Family
1966
"Our quiver is full."

a certain church that we would be called to pastor. He described the Findlay church in detail at least five years before we arrived there. What a confirmation!

In 1959 I was asked to be the keynote speaker at our General Convention in Joplin, Missouri. That same year, I was elected the Ohio District secretary-treasurer and had the distinct honor of serving on the General Board of the Pentecostal Church of God. The Lord allowed me to serve in helping new church plants and placements of ministries through my office. This was the special favor of the Lord and He graciously enlarged our sphere of responsibility and service to the body of Christ at large. Betty and I were also chosen to be delegates to the American Bible Society advisory board in New York City. Through these bi-annual meetings in New York City we were introduced to key world leaders in various denominations including the Vatican. It was a great joy and fulfillment for us to travel to New York at least twice a year for a number of years.

Our First Missionary Journey

In 1961 Betty and I traveled to Haiti and Jamaica to visit our first "sent" missionary couple, Jack and Betti Snyder from Findlay. We had a sincere heart to help the Haitians, and this was the first of many trips that we would make to Haiti and the Caribbean. One of our memorable trips to Haiti included traveling on the "Mission Possible" boat with the Snyders. The two Betty's decided to dive off the ship that was anchored about a mile off shore, and they swam safely ashore. Quite brave gals I'd say.

Jack Snyder was called home to Heaven several years ago after literally pouring his life into his beloved Haiti. Betti and her sons, Peter and Phil, carried on the work that included building and supplying schools for many thousands of Haitian children. Betti still lives and serves in Haiti with Phil. Her son Peter and his wife Lauren live in Kunming, China, where they have during the past thirty years established and built numerous schools and training facilities. I had the joy of traveling with Pete to many parts of Yunan Province where he built schools among eighteen indigenous people groups on the Laos-Vietnam border. Pete and Lauren are very dedicated to the work of the Lord.

In 1984, we introduced Pat and Pete Gruits, our dear friends from Bethesda Church in Detroit, to Haiti. Seeing the great needs, they were moved with compassion and literally "pulled up stakes" in Detroit to give themselves for many years to build a strong base in St. Marc and surrounding areas. The legacy of the Gruits in Haiti has included a fully staffed hospital and many other outreaches to the country. Pete Gruits has gone on to his eternal home, but Pat Gruits still blames us for getting her involved. She loves the people there, and she still maintains her vision for Haiti. Their ministry is called "Rhema."

Meanwhile, Back Home in Findlay

By the blessing of the Lord our church family kept growing, and we as pastors did as well. Revival was in the air, and the Lord reconnected us with our friend, Ern Baxter, a great Bible teacher, who regularly brought us rich and powerful truths from God's Word. We shared many insights and revelations together from the Scriptures as we "sharpened our axes." Brother Baxter and his wife, Ruth, spent many days in our home and were a great blessing to our family and to the whole church.

I remember vividly the vision that Ern shared with me with solemn tones as he arrived in Findlay in 1964. The Lord had shown him a vision of North America, particularly as a topographical map. On the surface of this map he saw emerging "Quonset hut" type buildings like bee hives sprouting up. He emphasized that they weren't spectacular buildings that would naturally draw people. He saw multitudes of people converging on these special areas, and heard them enquiring, "Where is the place of the anointing?" Ern described this as a mighty move of the Holy Spirit that he felt was coming. It was about the same time that the "Jesus People" movement was rapidly growing across America.

A little History about Findlay

I would like to insert a little of the spiritual history of Findlay, Ohio. Three major denominations were founded in this very conservative town. First, the Winebrenner Church of God was established there in 1942. A very notable member of that group was Mary Woodworth-Etter. She was the first woman (and perhaps the only woman) ordained by the Winebrenner Church of God denomination. She made her debut in ministry in the late 1800's. Her ministry was legendary, with many signs and wonders following. She was very active in revival meetings around Tiffin and Oberlin, Ohio, and at Heidelberg College, where God used Charles Finney to ignite the fires of a legendary revival. This was before the Pentecostal outpouring in Los Angeles in April of 1906. Incidentally, that phenomenal revival on Azusa Street was birthed the same day of the great San Francisco earthquake.

The Church of God-General Conference established Findlay College, which is now the University of Findlay. They also established Winebrenner Seminary which is still expanding in influence today. In fact, quite a number of the faculty and students from the seminary came to our church, and several received the baptism in the Holy Spirit. Out of this group the Anderson Indiana Church of God was established, which was non-charismatic. That group has also enjoyed extensive growth among the nations.

Birth of the Assemblies of God

In 1914 Rev. T.K. Leonard, who was a member of the Winebrenner Church of God, was introduced to the Pentecostal experience and received the baptism in the Holy Spirit. Rev. Leonard wrote the original charter for the first Assembly of God conference held that year in Fort Smith, Arkansas.

Findlay, Ohio, then became the first national headquarters for the Assemblies of God. America's first Assembly of God church is still located on Ash Avenue. It can definitely carry the name, "First Assembly." Brother

Leonard was a gifted visionary. He helped establish the first Assembly of God Bible school above a furniture store on West Sandusky Street. Some of our older members in our Blanchard Avenue church were related to T.K. Leonard. Several of his sons and grandsons were prosperous businessmen in our city.

Many of our seasoned saints remembered those early days well, including the time Aimee Semple McPherson arrived from Ingersoll, Ontario, to attend their aspiring Bible school above the furniture store on West Sandusky. Quite a number of leaders attended the Assembly of God Bible School in Findlay. Roswell Flowers, from a prominent Findlay family, became the first secretary-treasurer, and established the first national Assembly of God office in Findlay. He also helped publish the first *Pentecostal Evangel* magazine there.

Favor in Findlay

We felt like the Lord had planted us in a very fruitful place, a city of about 38,000 people. I knew with certainty that the Lord had sovereignly directed us there. He wrote the script, and we were making the movie. Every day was an exciting day of discovery in the manifold purposes of God.

God gave us much favor in that city. Shortly after we settled in there the mayor of Findlay and his family started attending our church. Several of his boys were saved, and some are still serving in the ministry today. Mayor William Carlin challenged me one day to bring our Sunday meeting out onto Main Street. It was in mid June of 1962, Findlay's sesquicentennial year. We agreed to go downtown on Main Street and bring our musicians and choir. The mayor had arranged for a large platform to be built right in front of the county courthouse, and a great crowd filled the street that had been blocked off. Marathon Oil Company produced thousands of song sheets so we could lead a great sing-along of old hymns and choruses.

We had the honor of presenting the Gospel of the Kingdom on Main Street several times in the years to come!

Many of these precious moments were recorded, and the history of that day was sealed in a time capsule that was opened recently at their bi-centennial after fifty years.

The Lord enlarged our sphere of influence with many of the surrounding cities as well. Our ministry was received and heard on two local radio stations daily in Findlay and its outlying areas. These were the days of the beginning of the charismatic renewal, and many precious families responded to the Holy Spirit. Once again we had a word from the Lord that it was time to rise up and build. We began to earnestly pray for a suitable location to build a new sanctuary.

Visit to Hungary

It was in the summer of 1964 that the Lord prompted me to visit and minister to our relatives in Hungary. All of my mother's relatives and many of my father's were still living under the communist-controlled government of Hungary. My brother, Bill, and another close friend, Pastor Bill Cox of Carey, Ohio, and I left Findlay on a great missionary adventure. After many delays and plane changes we arrived late at night in Prague, Czechoslovakia. The Czech Airlines eight-passenger twin-engine plane (built around 1940) to which we had been transferred was having serious engine trouble. The mechanics worked on it long into the night. We were finally cleared for take-off in a rain storm, and as we sat in the very small cabin, I noticed the altimeter was rising very slowly. My instincts, as a licensed pilot, told me that we were having trouble gaining altitude. This was confirmed as we flew very low by church steeples that we could see in the midst of lightning flashes. It was quite a terrifying trip for us all.

We finally arrived in Budapest, Hungary, at the Ferri-Hegy Airport. It was a dark and dismal place. We landed at about one-thirty in the morning. The immigration officials tried to be courteous and told us that our eight relatives, whom we had never met, had been waiting for us all day in the next room. One of them was a distant cousin, the captain of a paddle boat steamer that operated on the Danube River. My brother, Bill, and Bill Cox were cleared through customs, but I was detained. They explained that they could not find my visa letter of request, even though I was the one who had written the request for all three of us. I found out later that my Canadian passport had noted my occupation as "minister." They thought I was a minister of the Canadian government. They told me I must be detained. I spoke in Hungarian to the guards asking them to let Bill Cox stay with me in our "detention" room. Bill didn't speak Hungarian, so I said to him in English, "Is that ok, Bill?"

"Sure. No problem."

Then we were ushered in a small jail cell by a Russian soldier outside our window. (Hungary was occupied by the Russians at that time.) My brother, Bill, finally went with our relatives to their tiny apartment in Budapest. He soon discovered that they had only one bed. To his surprise seven of our relatives, including old Granny, crawled into the fold-down divan with him.

Back at the jail Bill Cox and I had a good night's sleep. The Russians charged me ten dollars for the accommodations. When I later realized the limitations of our sleeping quarters at the apartment I decided it was worth it. The next morning the chief immigration officer was embarrassed and apologized for the incompetence of her night crew officers and graciously stamped our passports. We discovered that the Lord had gone before us. We were given complete freedom to travel anywhere in that communist country. The Lord had ordered our steps and our stops because we sure could not have all fit in the one bed. Two more would have been too many!

We soon discovered that we were under constant surveillance, even by my own relatives who had been indoctrinated for years by their communist government. This was the first of many trips that we would make to Hungary, and eventually Betty and I would make our home there for an extended season of ministry.

We continued on our journey to several nations, including Lebanon, and from there we drove through Syria and Jordan into a very hostile setting on our way to the Israeli border. We were stopped at many check points, and the Arab soldiers always questioned me suspiciously because my name was Moses. However as we passed through the Mandelbaum Gate our Israeli immigration officer shouted, "Shalom, Moshe!" Apparently he too assumed I was Jewish. (I seemed to have a map of Israel on my face.) We joyfully but cautiously went on to have a delightful tour of Israel. It was a very exciting trip. The three of us baptized one another in the Jordan River. Actually we were dropped over the side of a row boat by our Arab guide who had tied a greasy rope around us to pull us back into the boat. We traveled from Israel to Athens and then on to Turkey. The Lord opened many doors of ministry along the way. I arrived home with a rekindled zeal to fulfill my heavenly calling and a fresh vision for reaching the nations with the Gospel of the Kingdom of God.

Moses and David Kiteley in Africa

Chapter Nine

Ministry in Findlay

Meanwhile our quest for a new church building site continued. During this time the Lord had directed me to an elderly gentleman with whom I had established a good relationship. He owned a very desirable piece of land, about seven acres, near our Blanchard Avenue church, and he assured me that he wanted us to buy it. Our church leaders were all excited as we proceeded to arrange to secure the property. I was delegated to go to the gentleman's home to sign the offer to purchase. While I was signing the papers, suddenly, my friend said, "Please excuse me. I am not feeling well." I was compliant and responded, "Don't worry. I'll call back later." The man had a heart attack and died a few days later. He had not signed the contract!

This development really shook me up. My wife, Betty, said to me, "Don't worry. God has something better." She went on. "What about that old house you showed me the other day on North Main Street?" I was completely taken off guard. "Are you talking about that old haunted house?" I had teased her a few days before about buying it for us to live in. Sometimes wives fail to appreciate our attempts at humor. "Well, we're pretty sure there's no one living there now," I concluded.

At that moment the Lord spoke to me and said, "Go there right now." I immediately left for North Main Street. The old house looked desolate. Weeds as tall as six feet covered the ground around the house, and junk was scattered throughout the property. The windows were broken. Curtains flapped in the breeze. The whole scene looked eerie and uninviting. Walking around the house I discovered that the side door was unlocked. I cautiously opened it. Upon entering I found a very strange old lady. At first glance I thought she might be dead. She looked like she had literally grown into the couch on which she was lying. I glanced momentarily at the dried-up carcass of a dead squirrel on the floor. Piles of rotting garbage littered the house.

The old lady seemed to come alive when I spoke to her. "Oh, Pastor Vegh, I know your voice!" She had a little wooden cabinet radio perched on her chest. She had over the years been a regular listener to our daily radio programs, and through the hearing of the Gospel she had received Christ as her Savior.

Mrs. Sherwood asked me, "Why have you come?"

I replied, "We are looking for property to build our new sanctuary."

"Do you mean my twenty-five acre bean patch out there?"

I was suddenly aware that this was divine intervention. One good door closed, but another door was opening that would prove to be the best. When God closes one door, He will open another, even if it seems like "hell in the hallway."

Several days later Mrs. Sherwood called us and said, "Get over here as quick as you can!" I thought she might be dying.

"Well, what about the bean patch?" I inquired.

"Oh, I have already called my attorney and he has drawn up the deeds. I won't sell it to you, but I will give it all to you for the Kingdom of God. Your new sanctuary will be in my bean patch."

That precious lady, because of our broadcasts, knew all about our family. She even recited the names of our children. She had never married, so she had no children of her own. She asked, "Would you adopt me as a member of your family?" She also said she would sell us her old house. (It was filled with antiques and fine china which she said she had saved for Betty.) Betty was to be her "Angel." I assured her that the Lord had arranged our meeting and, yes, we would adopt her and care for her for the rest of her life. She was 83 years old at the time. She lived with us for over three years, sometimes becoming confused and calling Betty "Mother." Betty and I bought her house on about 1.5 acres, and she lived in it while we completely renovated and remodeled it. Mrs. Sherwood lived to see the dedication of the new church, and for about three years she was a part of our family in our restored home. Betty cared for her with tenderness and compassion.

Betty and I had previously driven by the new Congregational Church building in Toledo several times, and I decided that we should build a similar structure. As soon as we had the deed to the "bean patch" I felt the Lord direct us to go to Toledo and look at that building in detail. When we arrived no one was there except the custodian, who just happened to be carrying out a massive display board with the architect's model of the church intact.

I said, "Sir, where are you going with that board?"

"To the trash. Why? Do you want it?"

"Yes sir!"

He placed it in my station wagon. "Oh, by the way," he said, "We have a complete set of state-approved church plans in case you are thinking about building something like this."

"We would be glad to take them off your hands if you would like."

We soon discovered that our land on North Main Street was a quarter of a mile outside the city limits, so we did not need a local building permit. All we needed were the state-approved plans which we had already received in Toledo. God's favor was evident, because He had sent to us a dear friend in Bob Marsh. Not only was he a member of our church board, he was also the Wood County Commissioner. The fact that he also served on the Cygnet Bank board helped make him a blessing indeed. We had all of the financing arranged in short order. Our general contractor was Gene Byrd who was one of my spiritual sons. Dan Kern was another skilled builder and church board member. Together with a great crew of workers they proceeded to build a beautiful building for the glory of God. Within seven weeks from the time we were given the land we started pouring the foundation. It was January of 1967.

The new Hope Temple Chapel was completed within a year and six months. Pastor "Mom" Beall and her son, Pastor

James Beall, helped us dedicate the new sanctuary in October of 1968.

Dr. Finis Jennings Dake (author of the *Dake's Annotated Bible)* held our first Bible Conference in Hope Temple. His grasp of the Word was phenomenal. During those days the Lord established a clear mandate in my heart to lay good spiritual foundations in the hearts and minds of the people so that the ministry in Findlay would endure for future generations.

What God Hath Wrought

During the sixties the Lord let us become a vital part of the charismatic renewal that permeated our area. This was also the time of the great "Jesus People" movement. Many hungry hearts were coming into our church from a variety of religious backgrounds. Catholics and people from other mainline churches came to be taught in our special catechism classes. The Lord had instructed me specifically in a vision to make sure that we laid good spiritual foundations in the lives of the people. We were so blessed to have the help and skills of men and women of God that came to us in these times of renewal and change. Paul and Eleanor Stern and the entire Beall family from Detroit were great inspirations to us. These anointed ministers helped us with our catechism classes and the *Understanding God* curriculum which had been written by James' sister, Patricia Gruits.

About this time, our brethren from the Pentecostal Church of God were not quite ready to embrace the charismatic renewal. They asked me very graciously to leave their organization, and I complied. The parting seemed to me to be mirrored in history. I left the fellowship, "even as Abraham left Lot." I said we would go because I knew how Abraham ended up. We had a very amicable parting. In fact, we gave them back the original building on Blanchard Avenue which is still operating today. To this day we maintain a good relationship with many of our Pentecostal Church of God brethren.

Awesome Days of Harvest

One of the things the Lord made very clear to me was that He would send us many new people, and we were not to check their labels. We were to disciple them by teaching the foundation classes and to lead them into the mighty infilling of the Holy Spirit. By the grace of God we fulfilled our heavenly mandate to make disciples and teach all people groups. Many hundreds came to know the Lord during those days. They came from various religious and cultural backgrounds to become blended and united together into a distinct and loving family. Fully thirty-five pastors from nearby churches came for water baptism and to receive the baptism of the Holy Spirit in our first year in the new chapel. Several hundred new believers that year who had been instructed in the Word of the Lord were baptized in water and in the Holy Spirit as well.

God was moving mightily, both at home and abroad, as I continued to travel to several countries and minister to many leaders and pastors. The Lord was preparing me for a far larger area of ministry than I could imagine. The recurring vision of His original call on my life was compelling me to explore ever expanding fields of service.

We had several outreach ministries to the surrounding cities. In fact, the populated area within a radius of about seventy miles around our city became a very fruitful field. We helped plant several strong works in that season of outreach. Many of those groups were part of our regular weekly catechism classes. Some of them drove seventy miles or more to be in class every week for the nine month course. Soon we realized that they were ready to plant churches in their areas. We encouraged them to build and we helped establish new buildings and new congregations as the Lord continued to add to us daily.

Our first commissioned team was Ernie and Kaye Weaver who were serving in our home church. Ernie had come to us from Kansas when he was twenty years old and was a faithful helper for several years. He was a talented pianist and choir director, and was skilled in preaching as well.[65] He had a Bible College degree and was developing as a preacher as well as a musician. We set our newlyweds, Ernie and Kaye, in as pastors of the Hope Temple Outreach in Petersburg, Michigan, in January of 1975. We had the privilege of helping establish a new church on the fifteen acres of ground that a member named George Loucks had donated. Within three years of the Weaver's transfer to Petersburg the people had built a beautiful brick facility with a 550-seat auditorium. They named the church New Life Tabernacle. Ernest Weaver served there as the senior pastor for fourteen years. The church has grown and prospered under the leadership of the Weavers, and then Dr. Kelly and Sue Silvers, followed by Tom and Nancy Rupli, and the current pastors who are doing a great job of reaching that area with the Gospel of the Kingdom. I was honored at their 35th anniversary in 2009 as the founding father of the work.

Fishing in a Fish Hatchery

The Findlay school superintendent, Bob Baker, spoke to our ministerial fellowship. He extended an invitation for us to teach Bible classes in the public high school to students who would voluntarily choose to attend. What an awesome opportunity! On a national level the Bible was being incrementally removed from the public schools, and the drug culture was growing it its place. I received a word from the Lord directing me to study Lamentations 4:1-5. The pervasive need for God that I saw among the students literally broke my heart. I could hear the cries of children who were seeking a word from God, spiritually starved and emotionally neglected. Amos the prophet also spoke of a day when there would be a famine for hearing a word from God[66] and how it would affect the youth.

---

[65] Ernie is also a very capable writer, and is now the editor and publisher of this book.

[66] Amos 8:11-13

I responded to the superintendent's plea for ministry to the high school students. I had no way of knowing how we would be received. The Lord gave us great favor and we enjoyed about five months of glorious revival in the school. My associate, Ron Beach, and I usually conducted three sessions a day, three days a week. It was like fishing in a fish hatchery. So many young people were ready to receive Christ. After about three weeks the students literally took over and shared their testimonies with one another. They were saved, baptized and subsequently some were called into Christian ministry. To this day they are still serving the Lord in various places. The school also asked me to do a full week teaching our catechism for their "Religions Week."

The Birthing of a Vision

During this time the Lord was birthing a vision in my heart for a large symphony orchestra for our church. This was not the norm in the churches with which we were related. I was especially led of the Holy Spirit to pray for an orchestra director. I found him at Findlay High School where we were conducting our meetings.

That man was Ralph Shell, a very gifted musician who also directed our Findlay Philharmonic Orchestra and served as the minister of music at the First Presbyterian Church. Ralph wasn't aware of my presence. I was hiding behind the curtains at the school claiming him for the Kingdom of God and especially for our Hope Temple orchestra. In a short time he was born again. His whole family came to know the Lord as well. His three children, Janet, Mary Jane, and Roger were all very talented musicians and were willing to serve in our church. This was the beginning of our Hope Temple Orchestra. Our anointed choir was directed by Dean Demos. We had many outstanding special event performances by a very impressive group of talented musicians and vocalists. Hope Temple became widely known as a church with great music, thanks especially to the skilled and anointed leadership of Dean Demos and Ralph Shell.

We felt directed by the Lord to open a Christian school at the church. Hope Temple Academy started as a kindergarten through high school program with the new ACE and ABEKA Christian curriculums. The great team of leaders and teachers excelled in the academic fields of study, but the greater emphasis was on developing anointed worshippers and skilled musicians. Our call was for the restoration of David's tabernacle that the Prophet Amos had foretold would develop in the last days.[67]

Our program included about an hour each morning for the students to play their instruments in worship and praise. (Almost all of our students played instruments.) Ralph Shell and Dean Demos were the primary teachers for the brass instruments. A large number of small children at one time played violins under the capable direction of Janet Shell. Five members of the staff had earned Master of Music degrees, and there were many other gifted teachers and assistants to support them. Ralph Shell is 95 years old as I write this, and he can still play his trumpet.

While we were enjoying a mighty outpouring of the Spirit of the Lord and having wonderful doors of ministry opening all around us in Ohio, I still had the recurring vision of the world harvest that the Lord had given me in my early days. My little raft was moving rapidly to new and exciting destinations.

---

[67] Amos 9:10-13

One day in April of 1970, while I was in prayer, the Lord told me that I would be receiving a call to minister in California. Shortly after that, I received an invitation from Allende, Mexico, to minister at a Bible school graduation and conference. I traveled to Allendé, near Monterrey. It was there that I met David Kiteley. We arrived on the same plane, landed at the same airport and were picked up by the same missionary. We were then assigned a room to share in the Horse Tail Falls Motel in Allendé.

The Lord knit our hearts together during those days and David invited me to minister in his home church in Oakland, California. His mother, Violet Kiteley, was the founder and senior pastor of Shiloh Church at that time. This was a divine encounter and we have since been traveling and ministering together in many countries for over forty years.

Moses, David, and John on a Forty-One Day Trip

On Christmas Eve in 1971 I bid farewell to my young family and also to our congregation. John Reynolds, one of our faithful elders, and I met with Pastor David Kiteley at the San Francisco Airport. We were on our way to visit seventeen countries in forty-one days. Our first stop was Auckland, New Zealand. David and I ministered there with Shawn Kearney, Rob Wheeler, and many other brethren on both the north and south islands. We traveled on to Australia, and there again the Lord opened a very effectual door for us. The Lord continued to confirm His word as we traveled through Asia, Indonesia, Vietnam (the war was still on), Cambodia, and then to Hong Kong.

The Vision Becomes Reality in Dacca

From Hong Kong our team traveled to Bangkok, Thailand. In Bangkok we were confirmed to fly on to Dacca, Bangladesh, where we were scheduled to speak to a pastors' conference. It was early in the morning when our plane descended over the Bay of Bengal, hovering over the seven heads of the Ganges River. The scene was exactly like I had seen it in my vision twenty-five years before. I said to David and John, "That's it!" There were the dugout canoes, the old paddle boat steamers, and great throngs of people on the shores. My heart soared with expectation. Truly God was fulfilling that prophetic vision that had sustained me throughout those years.

We arrived at the Dacca airport, mindful that our only flight out of there would leave within three days. Soon we were in a throng of thousands of people outside the airport and being herded toward a 1932 Peugeot. The driver was bearded, barefoot, and dressed in what appeared to be a loose nightgown. With a grin he quickly lashed our bags onto the top of the car and we crawled into the small automobile. The temperature was at least 110 degrees. We drove through masses of people, buses, sheep, goats, donkeys and more people, to finally arrive at our destination.

We pulled up to the conference compound of a major Pentecostal denomination. We were then told at the gate by the presiding officer that the conference had been cancelled. He offered us no reason and extended no hospitality. I learned later that the organization heading the event had not embraced the charismatic renewal. The director had heard that we were charismatics, so he cancelled the conference. We had traveled halfway around the world. I stood there with David and John, frustrated to say the least. The door seemed to slam right in our face.

We crawled back into the stifling heat of the old Peugeot and slowly backed down the long alley into the mainstream of traffic. There in the middle of the road one of our tires blew out. This was not one of our better days. The old driver scrambled under the car there in the middle of the road, with congested traffic and a maze of animals and buses all around, to jack up the car. He didn't have a crank handle, so he was turning the greasy screw jack with his bare hands. I noticed the spare was so thin that you could almost read a newspaper through it.

Something inside of me came to life and I said, "The Devil is not going to rob us of this awesome moment. Surely

God is doing something in this city of ten million people besides here at this compound." I went back to the main gate and shook it again. The same leader came out and I said, "Sir, is God doing anything in this city, besides here?"

He immediately responded, "Yes, I believe I know who you should contact." He opened the gate and led me to the phone, and connected me with a certain Swedish Baptist brother who was in charge of a large United Nations distribution office. Bengt Sundberg answered the phone and immediately we were bonded in the Spirit.

"Stay right there, Brother Moses," he assured me. "I will be there in minutes."

Bengt arrived in a new white 1972 Land Rover with air-conditioning! We hopped in, saying, "Just let us stay in this car. Don't turn it off for three days until we can catch the next flight out of here."

Bengt laughed. "No, you are my guests, and you will come to my house."

He happened to live next door to the Prime Minister, Sheik Mujibar. After a wonderful reception and refreshments Bengt said, "I know exactly where you are supposed to be."

"Take us there please."

We drove through desolate areas of the city, finally arriving at the Holy Cross Convent and Girls' High School. This very large compound was surrounded by high walls and it also included an orphanage.

We arrived at the great iron main gate. I shook the gate and the young gate boy opened it. When he saw us standing there he began to shout, "They're here! They're here!" We looked around and wondered who "they" were. Immediately we were ushered into the main courtyard, and we saw the "flying nun" Sister Margaret, come running out of her office toward us. She had her hands in the air and she was praying in a heavenly language. She told us that just three weeks before she had been in San Francisco in a Catholic charismatic conference and had received the baptism in the Holy Spirit.

Now she was weeping as she told us that when she received the Holy Spirit she was praying, "Oh Lord, how can we bring this wonderful blessing to our compound in Dacca?" One of the prophets at that meeting spoke up and said, "Don't fear. The Lord has already ordered men to appear at your gate when you return. They will come to you, and you are to receive them. They will bring the Holy Spirit to you all. When they come, you are to shut down all your activities, and call all your staff and leaders and guests into the chapel to hear what the Lord has to say."

Sister Margaret was ready. She ordered everyone, including the Mother Superior, nuns, priests, and our team (including our Baptist brother, Bengt) to sit down in the conference room and hear what the Lord had to say through us.

This was so much like the occasion in Acts ten when Peter was addressing the household of Cornelius. I began to share the vision that the Lord had given me as a youth. As I spoke the Holy Spirit fell upon all those present, including Bengt Sundberg. There was a Bengalese Seventh Day Adventist pastor who happened to come in and several priests and nuns, including the Mother Superior, who where all speaking in tongues. Great joy filled us all.

Sister Margaret had been in San Francisco three weeks before to receive the prophetic word regarding men who would be coming to her gate. We calculated that she left San Francisco the same day that we left from the same airport to start our journey around the world. We had been traveling three weeks in several countries around the world and now we were in Dacca. Sister Margaret had just arrived home a few days before we arrived. God is so awesome and the prophetic word is so powerful. God watches over His word to perform it. We found that God orders our steps and our stops. When the Lord closes one door He opens a greater door. The Hungarians have a saying: "If they throw you out the door, climb in a window." Little did I realize what an effectual door had opened to us in Dacca.

Sister Margaret prevailed on us to minister to their team for several hours. She also pleaded with us to send them another team as soon as possible. We were now on our way to a pastors' conference in Poona, India. Poona had the largest Jesuit community in the world, and many of these priests came to our conference there and received the Holy Spirit baptism. When we reported the good news about Dacca, the brethren there sent a team at once to continue ministering to the Catholic charismatic community. We were told that over one hundred and fifty leaders received the Holy Spirit during their initial visit.

The news traveled throughout India that there were "three angels" who had brought revival to the Holy Cross Convent in Dacca. We were told in recent years that hundreds of new churches have sprung up in India and other countries as a result of that initial outpouring of the Holy Spirit in Dacca.

David, John, and I continued on our journey to India, Israel, Hungary and England. We had traveled in seventeen countries in forty-one days, a journey that was wonderfully blessed by the Lord. The relationships that began during that journey are still vital to our ministry to this day. The Lord kept working as we shall see.

Meeting Khushi - From Dacca

It has been my privilege to minister in the International Ministers and Pastors Conference at Faith Fellowship with Pastor David T. Demola in Sayreville, New Jersey, for several years. One day in July, 2008, while at the conference, I was walking through the lobby of our hotel when I met a dark-skinned man who approached me to express his gratitude for my ministry to him personally during the conference. His name was Khushi.

"Where are you from?" I inquired.

"I am from Dacca."

"Dacca? Please tell me how you became a Christian."

Khushi responded, "I was a Hindu. One day while walking down the street I met a man whose name was Bengt

Sundberg who had recently received the Holy Spirit in a Catholic convent meeting and was now starting a church. I was his first convert!"

"Wow!" I exclaimed with delight. "I know Bengt Sundberg."

His eyes opened wide with an expression of great joy. "You! You are the Moses! Don't move. I must get my camera and get your picture. You see I have heard of you for over thirty-six years. You have prophesied over me here, and now I am so excited. You must come back to Dacca!"

In the meantime I had met Bill Simmons, a man whose family was a part of our first pastorate in East Alton, Illinois. Bill was five years old then. He is now retired from Shell Oil Company and is utterly devoted to world missions, especially in China and Bangladesh. Bill arranged our trip to Bangladesh in 2010. It was thirty-eight years after my initial visit to the compound. Khushi, who had heard my story, arranged for our meeting in Dacca on the same grounds where we had been "unreceived" in 1972.

A gracious new leader of the Assembly of God compound welcomed us, and he was very open to our coming. Bill Simmons, Chris Owens (a young man from San Clemente) and I were well-received. There were about fifty leaders and pastors present. For over four hours I rehearsed my story of coming to Dacca thirty-eight years before. With tears of joy we laid hands on all the leaders present, anointing them with oil and praying for a mighty revival in Dacca. We had a great meal together and were richly blessed by the warmth and reception of these dear men and women of God. The brothers begged us to come back soon for a city-wide conference.

Then Khushi took us back to the Holy Cross Convent. There we saw the same old iron gates. A sense of euphoria filled our hearts as we were lovingly received by some of the old sisters who had retained their zeal and passion for the Holy Spirit. They had been praying in charismatic meetings every week for many years and hoping that we would return. They hugged us and we rejoiced together for the wonderful revival that had started there and spread over Bangladesh where Khushi now oversees two hundred and fifty churches. God is so faithful to perform His word and to sustain that which He began. We have a standing invitation to come back to the convent and have a mass conference on the Catholic conference grounds. The last chapter concerning Bangladesh has not yet been written.

Our China Connection

Dennis Balcombe is our China connection. As a young man he had been sent out from Shiloh Church in Oakland to minister in China. He had a special prophetic impartation and appointment to China when he was sixteen years old. After serving in the army in Vietnam, Dennis moved to Hong Kong. The doors were not open for him to travel into mainland China yet, so he had settled in a little room in the heart of Hong Kong. Dennis was already busy planting a local church in the city. He was becoming fluent in Mandarin Chinese, the most widely-spoken language in the world. We were blessed and inspired to see his humble beginnings and to partner with Dennis and Cathy and their family for the ministry in China.

This again was a time of reflection on the vision that the Lord had given to me about reaching many nations with the Gospel of the Kingdom. Little did I know then that we would be traveling into China on many subsequent trips and ministering to literally thousands of dedicated leaders in the underground church.

On one of our trips into China with Dennis we took a group up to White Cloud Mountain outside of Ghangzhou, Canton. Betty and about thirty other believers were with me. David Kiteley had contracted with a communist entertainment park for a bus and driver. We were to travel to the top of Snow Mountain where two faithful brothers had arranged to meet us. These men were fugitives from the law, having been in prison for about seven years for preaching the Gospel. They had prearranged with Dennis to travel about three days on a train (with fake identification papers) and then to walk for the better part of a day up the mountain. These two heroes of the faith had prepared a "brush arbor" in the woods where we all met and prayed together with about thirty believers. Those brothers today represent several million new believers throughout China. We visited their work in Whanzhou and saw firsthand the powerful work that the Lord had done.

One more glorious experience was in November, 1993. Pastor Kiteley asked me to join his team of prophetic ministers to travel into selected villages in Anhui and Hunan provinces in China. Doug Balcombe, Dennis' brother, Sharon Balcombe (Dennis' daughter who served as my interpreter), David Kiteley and "Susie," another interpreter, made up our team. We traveled to Hefei in Anhui Province by plane, and then drove about twelve hours into the night in a badly worn old minibus. There was no heater and not one solid window in the bus. The air was freezing cold, and the roads were treacherous with snow and slush, yet we traveled on. "Sister Ding," a legendary woman of God who had endured much persecution, joined our team. We arrived around midnight to our first village and slept about four hours on wooden slats covered with a bamboo mat. It was not quite the four star Hilton, but we did see at least five stars through the thatched roof.

We traveled for ten days, constantly dodging the secret police (The People's Security Bureau). We traveled from Pangcheng to Nanyang, Tanghe, Wuyang, and Zhoukou. All of these villages were in Henan. Then we traveled to Lixin, Guoyang, near the Yellow River, where about 140,000 people perished in flooding in 1991.

We continued ministering prophetically every day in the villages to about three hundred leaders in each place. It was bitterly cold, but those predominantly young leaders were ablaze with the glory of God. For them the presence of God was worth the danger and the discomfort of their "illegal" meetings. Even chairs were a luxury. The participants were usually seated on a cold dirt floor.

I was awakened at about 4:30 each morning to the sound of powerful worship and prayer. I thought that perhaps I had died and gone to Heaven. Our tea time was about 7:30 am. Immediately afterward we taught the Word and ministered to each leader prophetically. Most of them were young people, and about seventy percent were young women. (Many of the older male pastors were in cruel prisons, and some had been martyred for the sake of the Kingdom.) We usually finished after dark with our main meal of Montou bread and a whole chicken (including the head and feet) in a bowl. Sometimes we were served a whole carp: head, tail, eyeballs and all.

Most of these leaders had traveled long distances. Many of them had walked or ridden bicycles over rough dirt roads. In fact, quite a few of them testified that the Lord had told them what village they were to travel to. They had no means of communication, but the Holy Spirit would tell them where our next meeting would be. They would start out many days in advance and arrive at our place of ministry on time.

The Heavenly Man

During our prophetic presbytery meetings in November of 1993, Brother Liu Yun, now famous as the "Heavenly Man," was assigned to be my companion in ministry. He prayed fervently. When I was exhausted after a long day of ministry Brother Yun would massage my shoulders and back. He was literally holding up my hands to minister. Each team member on average prophesied over at least a hundred believers a day. Our "sanctuary" was actually a chicken yard. Among our precious guests were several species of barn animals, including ducks, chickens, rabbits, and an occasional hog.

I felt that this was the "goriest" and yet the most glorious of any meetings we had ever encountered. The presence of God was unspeakably powerful. We continue to hear the marvelous reports of those dedicated leaders, and of the exponential growth of their churches, with participants now numbering in the millions. It is currently being reported that an estimated 35,000 people are being saved daily in China.

William Booth[68] said, "It seems that men are always looking for better methods, but God is looking for better men, and some of God's greatest men are women." Many of these brave souls had been imprisoned, beaten and isolated from their homes and families. But you will never meet a more cheerful group of victorious saints.

Those Chinese Christians didn't merely say prayers. They really prayed, and they prayed fervently. They read the Bible and believed it. No one had told them that Jesus did not heal anymore, so they healed the sick, cast out devils, and, oh yes, they raised the dead, all in the name of Jesus! (We heard of twelve documented reports of resurrections from the dead in that area where we ministered by these same young leaders.) We have countless reports of the supernatural Acts of the Apostles types of ministry conducted by these young firebrands for God.

"The people that do know their God shall be strong, and they shall do exploits!" [69]

We continued to hear many reports from those whom we had personally prophesied over of the amazing fulfillment of the prophetic word in their lives, with signs and wonders following. We finally returned to our destination in Hefei in Anhui Province and had to wait two days for our plane to carry us back to Hong Kong.

This young church, as in the book of Acts, is characterized by its simplicity and singleness of heart. The pioneer church under persecution is always vigorous and flexible. Over time it tends to became fat and short of breath through prosperity, or muscle-bound by human bureaucracy. No one can hear these reports without being convinced that Someone is at work besides mere human beings. The Chinese church is a perfect match to the one described in the preface of J.B. Phillips' translation of the

---

[68] the founder of the Salvation Army
[69] Daniel 11:32

book of Acts. Here we see the church as it was meant to be, a happy body of believers in its youth, valiant and unspoiled; a body of ordinary men and women joined in unconquerable fellowship on a level never before seen in China. They may seem uncomplicated and naive by our standards, but they are certainly open to God's every whispered command in a most refreshing way.

Chinese ministries are a vital part of my continuing apostolic journey and the reinforcing of that original call and vision that the Lord gave me. For several years I have had the honor of ministering to a variety of gatherings of Chinese pastors, both on the mainland and also in our annual pastors' meetings in Hong Kong. It is a great privilege to serve these dear saints who have totally sold out to Jesus and are fearlessly evangelizing their nation. Even the current communist government has had to acknowledge that the newborn Spirit-filled believers are a tremendous asset to China and her continued prosperity.

Moses receiving honorary Doctorate of Education and Training degree, Wenshan Teacher's College, Yunan, China, with Peter Snyder, 2001

Chapter Eleven *An Encounter with Destiny*

We were in a season of enlargement as the Lord continued opening many new doors of ministry for us back in Findlay. We were witnessing a very significant number of new families coming to the Lord. Among them were officials from our city and state governments. During this time we traveled with our family to Washington, D.C. along with our elders, Jim and Robin Sterling. We were to meet our missionaries, Graham and Pamela Trustcott, a New Zealand couple who were doing a phenomenal missionary work in northern India, and drive them to New York City to catch their plane back to India.

Tennyson Guyer was the congressman from our district in Findlay, Ohio, and he had arranged for us to meet key officials in Washington. President Richard Nixon was in the spotlight of the daily news reports with the Watergate political scandal. Tenny introduced us to two key officials: Max Freidersdorf and Bill Genader. These men were special liaisons between Congress and the president. They were very accommodating and showed us around Washington, giving us critical access to many unusual places in the halls of Congress and the White House. Jim and Robin Sterling, along with my own family, were staying at the Mayflower Hotel. John and Ann Reynolds, also elders from Hope Temple, had arranged to meet us at Monticello on Thursday. We had a good tour and as we left John and Ann, they said they were going to travel on to North Carolina and we bid them goodbye.

Our newfound friend, Bill Genader, had arranged for our meeting with President Nixon for Saturday morning. When we arrived at the White House we were told that the President had to cancel his meeting with us. He left us special tokens; Parker pens with his signature on them. We watched him from behind a screen as he hurried out the door to board his helicopter. Little did we know what was going on at that very moment. We were given special status with a secret service man to guide us (a born again Christian) who was told to take us wherever we wanted to go. We toured the Oval Office (where our son Marcus sat in the president's chair for his own photo-op) and then visited the cabinet room, the east room, and the libraries. The evening news that day announced that the "smoking tapes" had been found that would ultimately bring President Nixon's term to an end.

The Lord explicitly told me that we were to stay on in the Washington area. We had three adjoining rooms in the Mayflower Hotel, and with our doors open we could visit our four youngest children who went with us, and the Sterling and Truscott families as well. We prayed together as we listened intently to the news reports of the proceedings on the President's fate. Finally, on Tuesday morning [70] we decided to pack our van and drive our missionaries Graham and Pam Truscott back to New York City to catch their flight to India.

While the folks were packing, Jim Sterling and I decided to take the kids in our church van and drive over for a quick tour of the Smithsonian Institute. Jim inadvertently turned into Executive Drive which led us right to the main gate of the White House. Thousands had gathered to witness the final hours of President Nixon and jammed the walks and the streets. I was very eager for us to get out of this traffic

---

[70] August 4, 1974

mess, reminding Jim that maybe he made the wrong turn. As we rolled up inch by inch to the main gate, behold, there stood John and Ann Reynolds at the gate! I stepped out of the van to speak to them as Jim drove on, since there was no place to park.

"What are you doing here, John and Ann?" I asked.

"We are waiting for you, Pastor," they replied. "We were restrained by the Lord from going to North Carolina last Thursday. He instructed us to stay and pray, then He told us to write down what His message was for the President and to come here and wait for you. We knew you would meet us here. You are supposed to go into the White House and present this word." John handed me a scrap of paper upon which he had written:

"Mr. President, if you will openly repent of your errors, on television, I will restore your kingdom, (office) even as I restored David my servant when he repented."

I felt a strong witness of the Holy Spirit. In the meantime the Secret Service guard at the gate had noticed us, and came over and asked if there was anything he could do for us. "Yes," I said, "You can call Mr. Bill Genader. (I presented Bill's card.) It is very important." I knew that President Nixon was right at that moment (about 10:00 on that Tuesday morning) meeting with his cabinet and offering his resignation.

Bill Genader answered the phone. "Pastor, what can I do for you?"

"I have a very important message for the President."

"Come in at once."

The Guard said, "Do you know your way up to the main entrance of the White House?"

"Yes sir. We had a tour here last Saturday."

He then said that we could go ahead. He asked for no identification. He asked us no further questions. John, Ann, and I walked up the long drive to the front door.[71] I

---

[71] This was obviously long before 9/11.

remember seeing a tear on John's shirt pocket. Then, looking down on my own golf shirt, I noticed a major coffee stain, but there was no turning back now. The Marine guard saluted us and opened the door. Bill Genader was waiting at the door as we signed in, and he led us into a small sitting room, outside the Cabinet meeting room. This was adjacent to Rose Mary Woods' office. I handed Bill the note, and he was in shock.

He said, "Does God really speak to people?"

"Yes sir, and I want to know if you would be ready to hear His voice and accept Jesus as your personal Savior?"

"Yes sir!" Bill said, and then he voluntarily knelt with us as we prayed. He accepted the Lord Jesus as his Lord and Savior right then and there.

Bill then took the note to Rose Mary Woods, the President's secretary. Rose Mary carried the note to General Alexander Hague, the chief of staff, who in turn handed the note to Secretary of State Henry Kissinger. This all happened while we were sitting and waiting for Bill to return. Bill returned amazed. He told us what happened. Henry Kissinger said, "No! If the President would humble himself and confess his sins, it would be a terrible sign of weakness to the Russians whom we were confronting in a very real cold war." I found out that Henry Kissinger's rabbi had been present nearby and had already instructed the President that he had nothing to repent over.

Teddy White and others recorded that the President was so distressed the night before that he actually was praying to George Washington's portrait and instructing Henry Kissinger to pray also. Mr. Kissinger said that he did not know how to pray. President Nixon then asked him to kneel while he prayed. This was also portrayed in the television special "Nixon" years later. We were made aware that Billy Graham was posted thirty minutes away on call, but the President did not call him. (Did Henry Kissinger intervene?)

Satan intervened to block the powerful admonition from the Lord. Historians have repeated many times that if President Nixon would have admitted his part in the cover up on public television, the nation would have forgiven him. He could have ended his career in honor. This is one of those many "it might have been" moments in history. I wonder what happened to the note?

Bill Genader then offered to help us transport our missionaries, calling Dulles airport and arranging for a direct flight from Dulles Airport to India. God gave us awesome VIP favor at the airport. We were rushed right to the gate (no security checks) with a great amount of baggage, and there was no extra charge. We bid farewell to the Truscotts, then started our journey back home to Findlay in our church van.

We were awestruck by the mighty intervention of God, but saddened by the rejection of our leaders to the Word of the Lord. We heard on the radio as we traveled that Teddy White, the famous Nixon biographer, had told about a "delegation from Ohio" who had visited the White House.

Great and Effectual Doors

The Lord was very gracious in opening doors of ministry with our national leaders. On several occasions we were invited to attend presidential prayer breakfasts and various National Religious Broadcasters' meetings where we formed friendships with key congressional leaders. We even met President Reagan and other government leaders at these events.

In 1984 Betty and her friend Eleanor Stern were invited by President Reagan to join him at the White House for a conference with key women leaders. What a blessed time they had! We witnessed again a fulfillment of the prophetic word to us that the Lord would bring us before major leaders. This was a strategic time in our lives, where the Lord opened many doors of opportunity to minister on CBN and TBN as well. Christian television was gaining momentum and the Lord gave us His favor to share His word with many. I was asked to conduct seminars and leadership conferences for their staff meetings at CBN and at PTL where our son Marcus was directing television for Jim Bakker.

Seasons of Refreshing

The Lord kept drawing many pastors and leaders to Hope Temple who wanted to be filled with the Holy Spirit. The charismatic winds were blowing all across the land, even in many staid religious camps. We began to conduct special mentoring classes for local pastors on a regular basis, meeting and praying together in various churches each week. The Methodist Church near us in Van Buren, Ohio, had recently installed a new pastor. His name was Dr. Kelly Silvers. He started frequenting our Tuesday night catechism classes soon after we met. I was teaching on the doctrine of baptisms at that time. I taught that water baptism was much more than an outward sign of an inward work. According to Romans six, baptism means the sealing of our covenant as we are "buried with Christ to rise to walk in newness of life." In water baptism the sin nature, the "old man," is buried. We are set free to walk in righteousness. We receive a "circumcision of the heart,"[72] and we begin to walk in the liberty wherewith Christ has set us free.

One night around midnight I received a call from Kelly, and he said, "Moses, I must be baptized."

"When would you like to, Brother Kelly?"

He said, "Sue and I are ready now."

"Why?" I was not that eager to get out of bed in the middle of the night.

"I was praying in my church sanctuary. I came upon the baptismal font and realized that I was wrong in my concept of baptism. I needed to get rid of the font (which he did that night) and be buried in water with Christ and rise to newness of life."

So Betty and I got out of bed and met the Silvers in our chapel. Our baptistery was always ready. We had baptized many that year in water. Many also received the baptism in the Holy Spirit. All four of us went down into the water and I baptized Kelly and Sue that early morning. We all rejoiced in

---

[72] Colossians 2:12 Amplified Bible

the Lord's goodness and felt like we were baptized anew. We were refilled and refreshed in the Holy Spirit together.

Kelly and Sue were thrilled, but their church board was less than pleased. Shortly after their baptisms the board asked Kelly to resign. He complied and then joined our staff as a gifted teacher and associate pastor. Kelly Silvers became a very close friend and helped us in our outreaches. He eventually became the pastor of New Life Tabernacle, one of our church plants in Petersburg, Michigan. Kelly also traveled once with me to China and was a great source of strength and wisdom to many of our Hope Temple family members. Since then the Lord has promoted Kelly to heaven where we expect to rejoice with him throughout eternity.

God gave us many new friends in the ministry and our outreach continued expanding. We helped plant several new churches that reached from Marion, Ohio, to Dundee, Michigan. It was an honor to serve New Hope Center in Lima, Ohio, and Pastors Jim and Sheryl Menke. They have been and are a great source of strength and support to us over many years. These ministries also spawned new works in their areas of influence and today there are several thriving congregations, throughout northwest Ohio, expanding the Kingdom of God. To God be all the glory.

A Time for Enlargement

As the Lord continued to add to our church, the Lord was telling us it was time to enlarge our place of meeting. Our Sunday services were overflowing with people eager for a fresh word from God. We began to pray that the Lord would send us an architect who could help us develop the plans for our next phase of building.

One Sunday morning I was looking around the sanctuary and I recognized Bill Defibaugh, a renowned architect from Detroit, Michigan. I knew that he was an elder at Bethesda Missionary Temple. I felt prompted by the Lord to ask Bill to share a word. When he came forward he declared that God had "arrested" him the day before as they were driving south on Interstate 75 past Findlay. He was directed to drive into our parking lot and survey the present building. It happened that Betty and I were sitting in our yard next door and saw his Lincoln circling the building. The Lord had impressed Bill and his wife, Ruth, to get a room in a motel nearby, and there God downloaded the plans for our new expanded sanctuary. Bill shared that he was ready to provide all our plans at no charge. He would also help with the general construction, but we must do it soon. We all caught the vision. This was a very special moment. In a matter of days we called Gene Byrd, our faithful contractor. He was ready to move his family from Michigan and begin construction. Gene and Bill were soon working diligently on the project together.

The Lord had prepared the hearts of our great Hope family, and He continued to send us special families with multiple talents. Among them were Jim and Robin Sterling and their four children. Jim was a God-sent motivator of men. I called him our Bezaleel, after the man whom God anointed with engineering and craftsman skills to lead the construction of the Tabernacle under the leadership of Moses. Jim was a successful farmer, but he was so zealous of the house of the Lord that he actually hired someone else to do his plowing while he worked on building the sanctuary. His wife, Robin, only found this out after we gave him his due recognition at our dedication services. His diligence and talents were multiplied in many others, including our boys Tom, Marcus and Michael, whom he motivated to work with him on the building. Jim was tireless as our "man of peace." He was also on the bank board and became our main connection to the CEO of the bank. The financing for the new building came with delightful ease. God had touched the heart of the chief banker, and he closed the million dollar loan with a handshake. He and I formed a close friendship that has remained over the years. Jim Sterling is also a very dear friend to this day. Perhaps part of our connection is that Jim is my "Grandpa-in-law." (His son Gail married our daughter Becky.)

Jim Sterling and Gene Byrd made a terrific team, for which we shall always be grateful. Many dedicated helpers volunteered contributing amazing skills and talents. My wife, Betty, was also a tremendous help with her interior design skills. She recruited several dedicated and talented people who helped design and complete a beautiful church home. In fact, our whole family was involved. Each member contributed his/her specific talents toward the completion of the building as well as to the spiritual growth of the church body.

The sanctuary, with a large platform that could accommodate a two-hundred-voice choir and about seventy-five musicians, seated 2,200. The new facility also had a full basement that was used in the operation of Hope Temple Christian Academy. There were four stories of offices and meeting rooms on the north end of the building. Our sixteen-hundred-square-foot "Prophet's Chamber" was a penthouse on the top floor. It became a temporary home to many visiting ministers. We dedicated the new facility by marching from the chapel next door, led by a full complement of trumpeters followed by the rest of the orchestra members. The high praises of God filled the sanctuary as many friends and ministers celebrated with us. "Mom" Beall and her family were on hand again to help us dedicate our second new building in about five years.

Hope Temple choir, directed by Dean Demos
Hope Temple orchestra directed by Ralph Shell

Chapter Twelve

A Mandate to the Nations

We continued to maintain good connections with India after our initial visit in 1972, especially in the Poona area with the Graham Truscott family. In the fall of 1976 Jim and Robin Sterling joined Betty and me on a major trip that took us to India for ministry in Poona, Amednegar, and Pimpri. The Lord used our team to impart strength to the churches and to dedicate a new church building in Pimpri. While there we also helped ordain the new pastor. We had many exciting experiences in our travels there, including cobras in our bedroom ceiling tiles. Jim inadvertently took a sip of water served to us in Amedneggar, and it brought on a severe case of dysentery that lasted until after our arrival in Rome.

From there we traveled to Hungary to visit some of my many relatives. On our first night there all four of us slept on one sofa-bed at my old auntie's quaint house in Baja. It was the only bed in the house. Our hosts sat up all night in their chairs, tending the fire, and preparing our breakfast. The bathroom was an old outhouse located on the other side of the chicken yard. The trip was particularly interesting with the added obstacles of rain and slush. In the early mornings we heard the ducks and chickens squawking as they surrendered their lives for the ministry.[73] Our cousin, Pishta, a member of the secret police, was our chauffeur. He drove us to many meetings in their house churches. The iron rule of Soviet communism had transformed Eastern Europe from a thriving, prosperous area to a dark land of misery, poverty, and oppression. In spite of the beauty of the cities and the countryside, Hungary was a very depressing place.

Our next stop was Israel, and we had the joy of visiting many "off limits" places with our rented car. We kept getting lost, even sometimes when we were within sight of our hotel, but the Lord constantly protected us. A few guardian angels had to work some overtime hours when we crossed forbidden

---

[73] Translation: being the main course for the preacher's dinner.

borders along the Palestine area. It was an unforgettable trip.

The Lord continually confirmed His word to us regarding our original vision of reaching the nations with the Gospel of His Kingdom. Prophetic visions had depicted that Hope Temple was to be the center of a great "wheel" with many spokes connecting it to many nations and unreached people groups. We were witnessing that calling and the releasing of many new ministries emerging from our Findlay church home. We witnessed a marvelous move of the Holy Spirit at that time. Many new members, including Spirit-filled Catholics, were being added from a variety of denominations,. We lived in an atmosphere of expectancy.

The Birthing of the National Worship Symposium

It was in the spring of 1978 when the Lord awakened me early in the morning and spoke a word in my ear about calling for a "symposium of worshippers." The Holy Spirit directed me to go to II Chronicles chapter twenty. After a season of searching and prayer I called Dean Demos, our music director, and he came over with his tape recorder. The vision of a national gathering of worship leaders and musicians was birthed. The plans came together for us to host the first National Symposium of Worship. I heard in the Spirit the word "aria." I asked our band director, Ralph Shell, "Brother, tell me, what is an aria?"

He explained, "An aria is something like the capturing of the moment in music. Tell me your theme and we will write it."

"No, this must be a spontaneous production of the Holy Spirit."

Ralph replied, "I have never heard of any aria like that." But praise God it happened and we shall never forget that day.

Our dear friends, the Kiteleys, and their music team from Shiloh Temple in Oakland, California, joined with us in the planning and preparation of the gathering. About one hundred gifted musicians and worship leaders were invited from across the nation to teach workshops, play instruments, sing, and dance before the Lord. Hundreds of others gathered for three glorious days of excellence in worship and divine visitation. The Lord gave us anointed teachers who had heard the "joyful sound." Powerful teachings were presented on the origins of prophetic worship and the demonstration of the "song of the Lord" that forever changed our tone and mode of worship.

The prophetic song of the Lord was evident even in our children. It was quite common to have children as young as six who would come up spontaneously to the piano to play and sing a prophetic song. This kind of spiritual participation became the norm for our regular services, with a full complement of musicians playing skillfully. People came from far and near to see and hear this unique sound. Our choir and orchestra performances, especially at special seasons, were awe-inspiring. Great crowds would fill the sanctuary time after time.

Our subsequent annual worship symposiums were influential in releasing many anointed worship leaders that had a significant impact on many nations. We released a team to travel to Europe, led by Gordon and Marilyn Shoemaker who served as our youth pastors. Our daughter, Cathy, was a part of that team. They had a tremendous ministry season in Holland where a revival broke out among the Dutch Reformed people. The Living Word Church was established in Aalsmeer, Holland.

The Shoemakers went on to Budapest, Hungary, where they introduced praise and worship and the teachings on the restoration of David's Tabernacle to a small house group led by Sandor and Judith Nemeth. That Church grew exponentially in spite of communism's grip on the country. (That form of tyranny still prevails in many cities in Hungary today.) Today there are over a hundred sister churches connected to the main "Hit (Faith) Church" in Faith Park in Budapest, with a total of more than 12,000 people attending. It has been my privilege to minister to this great congregation on several occasions, and we have many friends in that fellowship. Our teams continued to travel throughout Europe and spread the good news of the Kingdom of God, especially releasing believers in high praise and worship.

Volumes could be written of those days and the subsequent symposiums we were honored to host. The effects of those times of impartation spread like a holy tsunami to many nations around the world.

I must share with you that with the great blessings and outpourings of God's grace upon us came severe testings. We were caught up in the ecstasy of the restoring of David's Tabernacle of worship. But I personally lost sight of the real intent of that scripture from the Prophet Amos.[74] I failed to see clearly that the glorious restoration of Davidic worship was to usher in a mighty harvest. There was to be a great acceleration of plowmen overtaking the reapers. We were very proficient and anointed in music and worship, but in retrospect I realize now that, to a degree, at times we worshipped worship.

The Lord God was graciously nudging my heart to see the harvest and His goal to reach multitudes of the unreached peoples of the earth. I was grateful for the talent, teachers, and performances of high praise in song, but the restoration of David's Tabernacle was not just about music and expressive dancing before the Lord. It was also about the restoration of divine order in the priesthood of believers, and in theocratic church government, with everything done unto edifying, decently and in order. Perhaps even more significant was the reality that David was not motivated by human ambition or empowered by military might. His strength was in the Lord. The Tabernacle was characterized by supernatural power, divine revelation, and effervescent joy. This kind of atmosphere was possible only because of the humility of the leaders and their wholehearted pursuit of God's presence and His approval.

---

[74] Amos 9:11-14

Chapter Thirteen

The Day the Storm Broke

The Lord had given us about twenty years of peaceful and expanding ministry in Findlay, and our church family was vibrant and growing. It was in February of 1979, after Betty and I had taken a few days off to rest and recuperate, when we returned home to find that a major insurrection had taken place. We can never forget the horror and pain that filled our hearts to be met with a large group of our congregation, led by one of my trusted associates, telling us that they had taken over. We were to surrender the church to them!

The seeds of discord and disintegration had already sprouted and were well watered. I had been cruising along on my little raft from victory to victory. We were in our third building program at Hope Temple. We were enjoying growth and delightful gatherings of worshippers in services and seminars. I thought we had a loyal, loving staff and congregation. I took my responsibility as a shepherd to heart. Even though a few were acting out of envy, spite, or personal ambition, I sought to be a peacemaker so that the lambs would be as protected from harm as possible. With a directive from the Lord to lay my staff down I surrendered to the dealings of the moment and looked to the Lord to be my defense. For many days I had little sleep or food. I was brokenhearted as I watched the "Absalom" drama unfold.

God in his mercy sent us help from many of our ministry friends. How grateful I am to this day for the sustaining power of those that God had put into our lives. Many ministers came or phoned to encourage us. I learned that there is a "voice" in God's rod. I was willing to receive correction, and to hear the message in this rod.

The Lord's voice crieth unto the city, and the man of wisdom shall see thy name: hear ye the rod, and (Him) who hath appointed it.[75]

---

[75] Micah 6:9

God was so merciful and gracious to spiritually sustain our family, as all of us were feeling the pain of betrayal. This insidious attack separated families and destroyed many friendships that had been forged over the years. The enemy had come in like a flood, but we praise God that most of those precious people have been restored as dear friends to us and to each other.

It was at times like these that I felt my little raft hitting the rapids and scraping against the rocks. I purposed to cast all my care upon Jesus, and to renounce all of the pride and ambition that had crept into my own heart. It was a season of deep healing of my heart, God graciously ministered healing and grace to Betty and our children. The end result was that we refocused on the purposes of God and resigned ourselves to His dealings. We were all "receiving correction," and it was more than just "getting the rod". I saw how important it was to own my own failures, and to trust God to deal with those who had sought to divide the body of Christ.

"And many will turn away from me and betray and hate each other. And many false prophets will appear and will lead many people astray. Sin will be rampant everywhere, and the love of many will grow cold." [76]

Jesus said that the sign of the end times in the church would involve betrayals. An enemy cannot betray you. The

---

[76] Matthew 24:10-12

word for betrayal, "paradidomi," literally means "to smite from beside." There are three steps mentioned in verse ten that naturally follow in sequence.

1. "Many shall be offended..." The word means "to depart from the faith." That is, the first step to division is the turning of our focus from God and His purposes to our own desires and purposes.
2. "..and shall betray one another." When we indulge in the sin of pride, we will blame and hurt others rather than love them.
3. "...and shall hate one another." It is the things we say about others that cause us to hate them, far more than the things they do. The person who does the betraying is far more likely to hate than the one who is betrayed. The tongue is a rudder that determines the direction of our hearts.[77]

Betrayal by friends is without doubt the most painful thing one can endure. I am reminded by our Lord when he spoke to the Apostle Paul of the night in which He was betrayed as being paramount in mind even many years after his death. He still related to the betrayal as perhaps being more painful than the scourgings of the cross. Jesus is greatly touched with the feelings of our infirmities. He also touched me deeply in the process revealing my own shortcomings, for which I am eternally grateful. The same God who comforts us gave us the comfort that we have been able to share with many of our brethren who have had similar experiences. I am so grateful to God that He dealt mercifully with our Absalom. After quite some time our former associate pastor, responded to the Holy Spirit, and in true repentance asked for our forgiveness. I am so grateful to God that by His grace He brought resolution and reconciliation to our family and to that brother's family before he passed away.

---

[77] Ernest Weaver, I Love to Tell the Story, Weaver Publishing © 1995

"Good judgement comes from experience. Experience comes from poor judgement."   **Ziggy**

"Success is not final, failure is not fatal. It is the courage to continue that counts."   **Winston Churchill**

After the Chastening: the Peaceable Fruits of Righteousness

I am often reminded of my early days at my grandma's house. Her humble little two room cottage was very plain and meager. She had no electricity or running water. When I entered into her sun porch kitchen I instinctively looked up over the door frame. There, sure enough, was the little red hickory stick, held up by two nails. Then I saw another object that was far more comforting to me. That was the little silver box with a paisley design on her dresser that held the camphor: Grandma's cure-all medicine. I remember the pain of the little hickory stick that brought me correction (usually far less than I deserved) and then the comfort of the camphor which she graciously applied. Grandma would take me over her knee after she administered the rod, opening the trap door of my long johns, and gently rubbed my bottom with camphor. It was always a pleasure to get the after effects. The Lord reminds us that no chastening for the moment seems joyful, but afterward it yields the peaceable fruit of righteousness.

The Power in the New Wine

Grandma was a typical Hungarian lady. My dad was a teetotaler. I never saw him drink wine except at communion. Grandma kept a vineyard, and now it was grape gleaning time. She carefully pressed the grapes and began the preparation of her "table wine."

I asked her, "Grandma, why do you drink wine and my parents don't?"

As she brought the grape juice to a boil on her old wood stove, she explained, "My dear, I am boiling the devil out of it." Then she proceeded to pour the processed wine into glass gallon jugs and cork them with a piece of corn cob. Later she carefully placed several jugs under her high featherbed.

Sleeping in that featherbed with grandma was a delight. It was so cozy. I really looked forward to coming down the road to her place each evening. Grandma would sing to me in Hungarian, from her *Songs of Zion* hymn book. She knew every song by heart. Then she would turn up the wick on the old kerosene lamp and open her Bible, usually to the end time chapters in Mathew 25, or Luke 21, and sometimes to the book of Revelation.

Grandma really believed in the imminent return of Jesus. She would remind me that when Jesus comes to take us away with Him, He would come with a great trumpet sound, with a severe shaking and a loud noise. Then she would remind me that we must pray always that we would be ready to go with Him. In my five-year-old mind, I knew that I had to do some repenting, because there were some bad things that I had done that day. Grandma taught me to read and write in Hungarian before I started school, and she would have me read to her out of her Bible. I remember reading that Jesus said, "Two would be sleeping in a bed, and one would be taken and the other left." However, I figured if Grandma started to respond to the upward call, when I heard the trumpet sound, I would just latch on to her several petticoats and ride up with her.

It was about three o'clock one morning when I suddenly heard a large explosion. The bed shook, and as I looked up on the wall. It was all bloody. I quickly felt for Grandma, but she was gone! I was terrified until I heard her praying in the kitchen, "Jaj Istenem!" (O my God!) Her wine bottles had exploded in a chain reaction. Wine and broken glass littered the floor and splattered up the wall. It was a disaster scene. Grandma was crying over all the precious wine that she had "corked too tight." Apparently she didn't get "all the devil" boiled out of it. I was so relieved that she was not injured, and I quickly helped her clean up the mess.

This event came back to me years later in a forceful illustration as I studied the words of Jesus regarding the new wine. Jesus reminded us that "new wine" had to be put into new wineskins that were "ready to be poured out."[78] The reason the wineskins (jars) broke is that they were corked. The new wine of the Holy Spirit is meant to be continually poured out. This glorious experience is described by Jesus.

> *"In the last day of the feast, Jesus stood and cried, saying, if any man thirst, let him come unto me and drink. He that believes in me as the scripture has said, out of his belly shall flow rivers of living water. This he spoke of the Holy Spirit which they that believe on Him should receive: for the Holy Ghost had not yet given: because Jesus was not yet glorified."* [79]

That prophecy was fulfilled on the day of Pentecost.[80] Many people exclaimed, "These men are full of new wine!" when they heard a hundred and twenty believers speaking in heavenly languages.

The Lord led us into a new season of harvest. I began to focus again on the purpose of worship and on building David's Tabernacle. It was the harvest that the Lord was most interested in, not our fine-tuned orchestras or vocal groups. It had to be an acceleration of ingathering. It was the time for the plowman to overtake the reaper. By the mercies of God we continued to see the Lord adding new families. Many of those who had been led away began to return, and we gladly received them. The Lord was applying the "camphor" after the rod!

Our children were now growing up and maturing in the Lord. Marcus, after graduating from high school, had enrolled as one of the first students in Jim Bakker's new School of Television Technology at Heritage, South Carolina. Our firstborn son, Tom, was attending Bowling Green State College. Debbie was working across the street at the Whirlpool Corporation. Cathy and Michael were enrolled in our Hope Temple Academy. Becky was our effervescent

---

[78] Luke 5:38
[79] John 7: 37-39
[80] Acts 2:15

receptionist at Hope Temple. Betty was faithfully serving the Lord and our family. We were all glad to be together for our evening meals and for our times of prayer and the word. All of our children loved to worship the Lord, and most of them were involved in our music ministry. Once again we began to sense a new season of fulfillment of all that the Lord had spoken to us prophetically over the years.

My little raft that I saw frequently as I prayed was often stuck in murky waters, or beaten against the shoals of life. At times we all drank from the bitter cup of grief and entered into the deep valley of the shadow of death. There were also many tense moments in our own lives. I was trying to function as father, husband, and pastor. In retrospect I realize that so much of what I was involved in was not as important as caring for the needs of my wife and children. During that time I was preaching three times each Sunday, at least four nights every week, and teaching at home and at outreach meetings in various towns.

In those busy times my little raft was actually airborne. I was traveling extensively to other nations on mission trips. I realize now that I failed to set my priorities with God's wisdom. I should have prioritized my time with my wife and children more. I have repented and can only say it was because of my sweet wife, my devoted  companion and faithful mother to our children, that we survived. Betty was always concerned about me, not just about my ministry and success. She served and loved with excellence both in home and in the church. She faithfully attended every service with our children and graciously ministered to everyone with her characteristic smile.

Betty's hospitality was a legend among ministers of renown; including the Kiteleys of Oakland, California, the Happy Goodman Family, Ern and Ruth Baxter, C.M. Ward, the Doug Oldham family, the Garlingtons, and many more. Our houseguests would always love to join us for some of Betty's chicken and dumplings and her exquisite desserts. Many happy hours were spent around the family table with all our children soaking in the many stories from men and women of God, including Rachel Titus. The residue of anointing received from being with our ministry guests remains with our children to this day, for which we are so grateful.

Our children thrived on our Sunday after-church (late) hours and frequent trips to Bill Knapp's restaurant. Writing excuses on Monday mornings for missing early school classes became almost a ritual. Betty's labor of love and gracious hospitality touched multitudes over the years, and some of them on occasion still remind us of the great times we shared in Findlay.

Hope Temple was a family, and the Lord gave us so many precious friends and spiritual children with whom we are eternally knit together. We had a great group of men that we called "Yokefellows" whom we mentored and established in the Word. Out of that group we helped train and encourage many faithful servants who served the church as elders, deacons, and in various ministries of helps. Our associates, teachers, and elders were also dear personal friends. Many of them remain so to this day. Hope Temple's deep commitment to fellowship as a family was almost legendary. We had great "pot-blessed" dinners. Some of the best cooks in the world were in our Hope Temple family. They are indelibly etched in our memories and forever appreciated.

Chapter Fourteen
Beginning

Shiloh's Humble

Shiloh was birthed under the direction of the Holy Spirit by Violet Kiteley, a mighty woman of God. Her initiation to Oakland, California, is a powerful and inspiring story. In 1964 Violet drove her old English Austin from Vancouver, B.C., to minister in a little church in Oakland. She soon found that her host had several weird doctrinal positions, so she decided to leave town. Her resources were limited, but she was determined to make it to Detroit, Michigan, to visit the Bethesda Missionary Temple. It was an almost unrealistic objective since the old Austin had some serious mechanical problems. She inquired about available mechanics and headed to the repair shop.

In the meantime a woman who lived nearby was desperately praying for her friend who had been paralyzed in a skiing accident. She heard the Lord telling her to "follow that old Austin." She followed in her Cadillac right into the repair shop behind Violet. The woman overheard the mechanic say that he could fix the car, but it would take several days to get parts. Violet then heard the lady say, "It's all right. You are to come with me." Violet sensed it was God supplying her with a place to stay, so she went with her.

They drove directly to the beautiful home of the paralyzed lady. Several friends were gathered around her bed. Violet declared the word of the Lord over her and prayed in simple faith. Immediately the woman leaped out of bed. The shouts of praise so alarmed the neighbors that one of them called the police. When the police came in they were informed of the miracle. One officer said, "Lady, come with me." Violet did not know that her "arrest" was going to be the beginning of an ongoing miracle in Oakland.

The policeman had an invalid wife at home, and he took Violet to his house to pray for her. God miraculously raised up that woman as well. The police officer then said, "You must not leave town. I will rent a place for you to have meetings in a store front on MacArthur Boulevard." This was the beginning of Shiloh Church. Today Shiloh is a dynamic group of believers from many nations.

Pastor Violet Kiteley later established Shiloh Bible College that has trained many skilled and anointed Christian leaders and pastors. Their ministry school alumni are influencing multiple nations to this day. The pastoral mantle was passed from Violet to her son, David. He and his wife Marilyn have done an admirable job as senior pastors at Shiloh for many years. David has also earned the respect of his community leaders and civil government officials. He is the personal confidante of mayors, police and fire chiefs. He is the president of a large pastors' fellowship, and he wears many other ministry-related hats as well.

David's son, Patrick, and his wife, Marlena, are now the senior pastors of Shiloh Church. They have three beautiful children. Under Patrick's leadership the church has more than doubled in membership. David and Marilyn's daughter, Melinda, and her gifted husband Javier oversee ministry to about one thousand children each week. Javier also pastors the Hispanic church that meets for the fourth service each Sunday. In addition, he is a supervisor on the prestigious East Bay MUDD water board. They also have two lovely children.

The Shiloh Miracle

Pastor David Kiteley and his family were and are very close to our hearts, and he was a frequent guest preacher in our Findlay church. We also enjoyed reciprocating ministry and fellowship to members of other churches in meetings over the years. All of our children were greatly blessed and inspired by their trips to Shiloh, especially at the Shiloh Mission Springs camp meetings.

In 1980 David had invited me to share a word to his leaders who were ready to build their new sanctuary. I asked Jim Sterling to join me. We arrived in Oakland and shared in their board meeting regarding their plans for building the new church sanctuary. Jim and I both sensed that the proposed building plans would not be adequate. The plans did not allow enough room for the expansion they would be needing in the future. We felt that God had something better and greater in mind.

We were staying with Jerry Mockma and his wife, Evelyn, who were seasoned and loving elders at Shiloh. Jerry was also captain of the Oakland Fire Department.

Jim and I tried to sleep, but we could not. Around midnight I felt a strong direction from the Lord to arise and drive to a particular building I had seen on a previous trip. We slipped out into the night and found the location at 3295 School Street. Jerry Mockma, along with his firemen, was fighting a fire that was raging down School Street at the same time. It was the old African Methodist Episcopal Church.

We found the Ahmes Temple, the central home of the Oakland Masonic Lodge. The building was very large and on a two acre fenced lot. The gate was locked, but we laid hands on the fence and prayed as we walked around the facility. I felt strongly that this would be the new location for Shiloh Church.

It was now early Sunday morning. I needed a little rest because I was scheduled to speak in the morning service. Jim and I were both ecstatic. We could hardly wait to inform Pastor David about our nighttime excursions. Pastor David was very kind. He gently informed us that the building was not for sale. It had been pulled off the market.

After the service I asked David to at least drive us by the place before we had our lunch. He obliged, or should I say, indulged us. When we arrived the place was packed with people. They were having a square-dance competition in the gymnasium. I went to the side door of the gym and knocked loudly. The doorman asked us what we wanted, and we asked for permission to see the inside of the building. His immediate response was, "Why don't you buy it"?

"We will," I blurted out.

"Ok, you can look around. I will arrange for you to meet the Imperial Wizard. He's in charge of the sale." We set a meeting time for Monday morning at 9:00.

Pastor David, his administrator, Steve Steinberg, Jim and I met the Imperial Wizard at the appointed time. He was already very heavily "lubricated."[81] (We soon discovered that there were eleven bars in the building.) Jim gave him the secret handshake that he had learned as a Mason many years before, and Mr. Suntag responded with a hearty, "Well, what will you give me for the building?" It had been appraised at between two and three million dollars. Brother Jim said, "We will give you $850,000." Mr. Suntag's face lit up with delight. He sealed the agreement with a handshake and gave us a closing date. There was only one problem. Shiloh Church had only about $50,000 in their bank savings account, and the bank had said they would not make any loan for a church building.

It just so happened in the providence of God that three weeks before this I had met Mr. Bob Bee. Bob was the twin brother of Janet Edwards, the principal of our Hope Temple Academy. Bob had told me at the wedding of his nephew in Findlay where we first met to call him if I needed anything while in the Bay Area. That day we needed him, because he was the vice president of Wells Fargo Banks International. He graciously responded to my request for a meeting, and we met in his penthouse office. Bob then invited us to the posh Bankers Club for lunch, where he was not supposed to conduct any business. We hailed a taxi. Bob apologized for not having cash to pay for the ride. (Apparently bankers of his caliber rarely carry wallets.) I was glad I had mine. After discreetly reviewing Shiloh's financial statement (under the table cloth) he shook hands with us and said, "Yes." He agreed to arrange for a loan of one million dollars. He was leaving for England in a few days to become the governor of a large consortium of banks, but he was available that day. God's timing is perfect.

---

[81] drunk

The local branch bank manager that Bob Bee assigned to carry out the loan came to visit Shiloh Church later and accepted Jesus as his Lord and Savior. Shiloh is still today operating in that renovated and expanded building and continues to have four services on Sunday to accommodate the thousands of worshippers in their multi-racial and multi-cultural congregation.

Washington for Jesus, 1980

It was during the 1978 Shiloh Church Camp at Mission Springs, Santa Cruz, California, that God spoke prophetically to John Gimenez regarding calling American Christians to Washington, D.C., for a day of prayer and fasting for the nation. Pastor Violet Kiteley was given a prophetic word of wisdom for John that we were to gather by the thousands on the mall in Washington, D.C., in a display of Christian solidarity. Miraculously it happened on April 29, 1980, and well over seven hundred and fifty thousand[82] believers gathered from every state and from other nations to worship God and pray for America on the mall. John and Anne Gimenez were used mightily by the Lord to bring about a display of unity in the body of Christ, and impact our nation for righteousness.

The day before the rally the area was plagued with cold rain and thunderstorms. The forecast for that Saturday was clouds and rain all day. Pastor Jiminez went to the microphone at six o'clock in the morning. The enormous sound system vibrated with the sounds of his prayer for better weather. Immediately the rain stopped. That day Washington D.C. enjoyed a beautiful clear sky with a temperature that reached an astounding 72 degrees. The national weather maps showed heavy cloud cover and rain completely surrounding the D.C. area, but the day was perfect for God's crowd. Many who brought large trash bags to use as potential covers for sitting or for makeshift raincoats gathered what little trash they could find and

---

[82] Most estimates placed the number at over one million.

deposited them in the available bins. After a full day of praise and preaching the Washington Mall was probably the cleanest it had been in decades. There was no violent crime in the D.C. area on that day. In one of the world's most dangerous cities, detecting only a purse snatching or two made it the easiest work day on record for that large police force.

Washington for Jesus, April, 1980

We were honored to be a part of this mighty effort and to share a word before the multiplied thousands on the mall. We took bus-loads of musicians and worshippers from Hope Temple. God smiled on His people that day and without a doubt it was the turning point of the election that year. Ronald Reagan, one of our greatest presidents, was elected over Jimmy Carter. Dynamic leaders from many Christian denominations participated in this historic gathering. We witnessed a great fulfillment of our Lord's prayer recorded in John seventeen when we saw so many become one. History will forever record this as a watershed moment. The reverberations from that day are still being felt throughout the nation.

It was shortly after that time that I was invited to be a representative of Pat Robertson's Freedom Council. I was asked to oversee six mid-western states. Ted Pantaleo was the general director. He opened the door for many wonderful connections with dedicated servants of God who were committed to bringing unity and change to our nation. I traveled extensively in those days calling for intercession and unity in the body of Christ. Our dear friend, Doug Kelley, from Montana, was over the Freedom Council in the northwestern states. David Kiteley presided over west coast states. Each of us traveled extensively to encourage churches and pastors to become more actively involved in changing the spiritual dynamics of our nation.

During those days Doug Kelly, David Kiteley, and I were invited by Pat and Dede Robertson to be their guests at their Blue Mountain Resort in Virginia. These were very strategic days meeting with Dr. Robertson, Ted Pantelano and the new director for the Freedom Council. We could see the "handwriting on the wall" relative to the demise of the Freedom Council as we knew it. At that time Pat declared that he would be running for the office of president of the United States. The Christian Coalition evolved under the leadership of Ralph Reed and engaged in the daunting task of trying to win the election. We knew that the Lord was bringing about new directions for our lives and for the nation.

Our son, Marcus, became very involved with the Freedom Council during those days, and he took over my position as director of our region. Marcus was brilliant in that position. He had ability to motivate people and was a great asset to Pat Robertson in his quest for the nomination. Marcus also worked on the re-election staff for Governor Rhodes of Ohio. While working in Columbus, Marcus was on staff at World Harvest Church, and was instrumental in helping Pastor Rod Parsley design and build their new edifice. Marcus is still honored at World Harvest Church for the devotion and skills that he displayed in helping this great ministry succeed.

Chapter Fifteen

Gleanings from My Treasure Chest

It was amazing to live in the unfolding vision that God had implanted in my spirit early in life. Just watching the hand of the Lord on our children as they developed into their respective callings was richly fulfilling. Each of them was discovering God's purpose in his life, and they all responded to His call. All of our children received powerful prophetic impartation by anointed spiritual leaders. Their individual journeys often took the "scenic route" and caused us some concern. We learned firsthand about the old adage that gray hair is inherited. We get it from our children. Ultimately God came through and we frequently marveled at His mighty grace and perfect timing in each of their lives.

Through many trials, temptations, detours, and delays, we have come this far by faith as a family. The path was not always easy, we were not always compliant, but God in His awesome grace has brought us through it all. Our love for the Lord and for each other has increased over the years. We are so grateful for the many friends that God has put in our lives who have supported us faithfully and prayed for us diligently.

I often think of our old friend Jamie Buckingham, a prolific writer and speaker, who said, "When you see me I want you to see a bumble bee. I am like a bumble bee that flits around from flower to flower, gathering nectar, and then distilling it into honey." I also have gathered much nectar from so many anointed teachers and inspirational writers over the years. What you are getting in these *Chronicles* is a distillation and compilation of so many "bumble bee" trips.

I have discovered that the entrance of God's word always gives us light. This word *entrance* literally means "cutting a sharp line" that opens a furrow into which the seed of God's Word drops and germinates. So the word of the Lord kept coming into my life. Many times in the night seasons the Lord would quicken me with revelation. I would arise and head back to my little study. It was a sweet asylum, a place of repose and safety for me. There I was surrounded by my beloved library. (Note that this was long before the wonders of computer science.) There I would dig deeply into the veins of revelation and endeavor to adequately write in ways that would capture the essence and fragrance of the illumination of the moment. I would recall the early days when the Lord opened to my spirit His word in Psalm 32:8-10 when I was in Brantford, Ontario. He assured me that He would "guide me with His eye." I also remember the day when He spoke to me from Job 32:8, while driving our old 1928 Chevy truck to the granary, about the inspiration of the Almighty that gives me understanding.

Words are inadequate to describe the flow of inspiration and revelation that I discovered dwelling in the secret place of the Most High. Of course, spiritual inspiration can be and usually is progressive. For example, many times I would pick up a key thought, and then instinctively a "chain reference" in my mind would take me from Genesis to Revelation in quest of confirming and expanding on the delightful truths in the passage. Inspiration would motivate me to study so that I would progressively see more light. *"In Thy light shall we see light."* [83] But revelation is usually like an instant flash. In a few seconds the Lord would download the whole concept in detail. My spiritual treasure chest "hopper" was filled in this manner time after time.

I would like to invite you to discover this exhilarating moment daily, for that is what the Lord wants for every one of us. He wakens me morning by morning, and He opens my ears to hear revelation. God wants to speak to you this very day. He who seals my instructions by giving me a word in season wants to do the same for you, whereby you can strengthen the weary. Revelation truth always demands a right response, or that same revelation can lead us to self deception.[84]

---

[83] Psalm 36:9
[84] James 1: 22, Isaiah 50:4-5

God is Not Giving You the Silent Treatment

God began to lead me into a deeper flow as my little raft proceeded down the stream of time. One day I was sitting in my study and I opened the Word to Mark chapter four. The parable of the sower is the first of four parables recorded in this chapter. I was particularly drawn to verses 13 and 24 (in the Amplified Bible) that showed me that this parable is the "Rosetta Stone," or the key to understanding all the parables of Jesus. I discovered that the power is in the seed. That seed was first planted in me, and then I became the seed planted by my Lord in strategic places. I was expected to conquer my environment and bloom where I was planted.

You are responsible for your depth in God. God is responsible for your breadth. You are not to give your energy to expanding and promoting your ministry, but simply to add to your faith virtue, and to virtue knowledge, and so on.[85] Promotion comes from the Lord,[86] and not from man. Any way He moves you is a promotion.

A prophetic "Now" word came to me as I was writing It was the Spirit of the Lord, that same Spirit who spoke to me as a fifteen year old boy driving our old truck, saying, "But there is [a vital force] a spirit [of intelligence] in man, and the breath (inspiration) of the Almighty gives men understanding."[87] I am inspired to tell you that God is getting you ready for that which He has already made ready for you! Your eye hasn't seen it; your ear hasn't heard it. This was by the inspiration of the Almighty given to Isaiah the prophet, "For from old no one has heard nor perceived by the ear, nor has the eye seen a God besides You, Who works and shows Himself active on behalf of him who earnestly waits for Him!"[88] Paul picks up on this awesome word and brings it down to us in a timely pronouncement declaring, "But to us God has unveiled

---

[85] II Peter 1
[86] Psalm 75:6-7
[87] Job 32:8
[88] Isaiah 64:5 Amplified Bible

and revealed them by and through His Spirit for the [Holy] Spirit searches diligently, exploring and examining everything, even sounding the profound and bottomless things of God [the divine counsels and things hidden and beyond man's scrutiny].[89]

The essence of this word was a divine instruction to call us to a confrontation with our awesome God. We are being surveyed by the great Architect who said "I will build my Church."[90] He has come suddenly among us in this day and He has come to lay the "Plumb-line" on us all. Our Lord is checking our foundations, our motivations, and our commitments. The question is: Who do we say God is? Are we being seduced by the 'god of open options" that is represented by the challenge given by Elijah to Israel on Mount Carmel?[91] If God is God then let us serve Him. If Baal is God, then serve him. Baal represents the "god of open options." They answered not a word! Your indecision is a decision to bow to the "god of open options." This spirit of indecision typifies the Prophet Joel's vision of "multitudes in the valley of decision."[92] This narrative begs for a response!

How long are we going to stumble, halt, and hesitate, being caught between two decisions? The Lord is confronting us with *now* truth. Are we ready to declare unequivocally that Jesus is Lord to the honor and praise of the glory of God? I believe this is the moment of truth for multitudes that have named the name of Jesus, and have been numbered among the seekers of truth, or even many of those who are caught in the mainstream of traditional religion. So many want to keep all their options open, but this is a deception that keeps you from total abandonment to our Lord Jesus Christ. He demands a total renouncing of self and sin, and a complete yielding to His sovereign command. The Lord is raising a whole new generation that will be command-controlled and voice-activated by the word of the Great

---

[89] I Corinthians 2:10 The Amplified Bible
[90] Matthew 16:18
[91] II Kings 18:21
[92] Joel 3:14

Shepherd. Multitudes of A.W.O.L. believers are being summoned by the Lord of the harvest, many who have had a genuine call to service. This call is "irrevocable." [93]

Are we ready to pledge allegiance to our Lord Jesus Christ, and renounce the "god of open options" who is declared to be the god of this world. The Lord whom we have been seeking is coming suddenly to His temple (that's us). His eyes as a flame of fire are assaying the true heart and confession of His Church. He is coming now in judicial majesty "to sit," which is a judicial term. He sits on His *Bema* seat, and He surveys with sovereign accuracy the whole core of our beliefs and our allegiance. He says, "Can two walk together unless they are agreed?"[94] The Infinite Creator of the universe declares, "I cannot change." He is calling for a total commitment to His lordship. No longer are we to "serve the god of open options." The Lord is coming suddenly to His temple, to His church, and to His pastors before He comes *for* his church.

I heard the Lord speaking to me about a "time for re-alignment." That word brought back memories of our early days in Findlay. Ern Baxter was speaking at our little church on Blanchard Avenue. As the word of the Lord came forth in revelatory power, I felt such a powerful "shift" coming. Then I saw in a vision a great cable wrapped around our building. Something like a large bulldozer was connected to that cable, and it was squaring the building, pulling it into shape and back on its foundation. I sensed the tension and shifting that was being felt by the whole church body. Then the word of the Lord came to me saying *"I am setting a plumbline in the midst of my people, I will not pass by them anymore."*[95] He is not going to let our shoddy work pass his scrutiny. Jeremiah had to tear down before he could build again. *"See, I have this day appointed you to the oversight of nations and of kingdoms*

---

[93] Romans 11:29 Amplified Bible
[94] Amos 3:3
[95] from Amos 7:7-8

to root out and pull down, to destroy and to overthrow, to build and to plant."[96]

> "No matter how great the pressure gets, never let it come between you and God. Let pressure move you into God."
> Hudson Taylor

It is time for the Spirit of Grace to come mightily on my people the Lord is saying to me. His people shall offer themselves willingly in the day of His power: in the beauty of holiness and in holy array out of the womb of the morning to Him will spring forth His volunteers, young men who are as the dew of the morning![97] This powerful word assures me that a whole new generation of youth is ready to respond to His mighty influence that is even now being felt around the world. Your sons and your daughters will respond, and they shall begin to boldly prophesy the clear word of the gospel of the Kingdom. They will willingly renounce the 'god of open options."

This is God's time to come among us and inspect His building. He is setting His plumbline on all that we call "church." He is not only getting an accurate reading, but He is already bringing the remedy for our procrastination and drift from the foundational truths. He is bringing alignment to the body of Christ. We are being called to a moment of truth; a moment when multitudes are being stirred by holy compulsion in the valley of decision.[98] This indicates a serious shaking, sifting, churning, and threshing that is even now taking place. The Lord is calling for a fresh commitment to His calling. Jesus is exposing the "god of open options" that has mastered so many of His children in this epochal moment of history.

---

[96] Jeremiah 1:10
[97] Psalm110:3
[98] Joel 3:14

So many pastors that are very near our hearts are being tested. The winds of adversity are trying their very core beliefs. Many are fatigued, and some are even fainting, being depressed beyond measure. This is clearly portrayed in Daniel's prophecy.

"The people who know their God shall be strong, and stand firm and do exploits. And some of those who are wise, prudent and understanding shall be weakened and fall, to refine them and to purify them." [99]

Remember the words of Jesus to Peter. *"Simon, Simon, Satan has asked for you, (and all of you) that he may sift you as wheat, But I have prayed for you that your faith would not fail!"* [100] Satan may take you to the brink of overthrow, but your faith will not be eclipsed. You will not fail the test when you are "converted;" then you are to strengthen your brethren."

Since God is God, we must believe that He is God and that He is a rewarder of all who diligently seek Him. Our God so loved that He acted. He gave us His only begotten Son. We must deny the "god of open options" who plagues us with questions. What school shall I attend? What is my elective? Shall I be married or just co-habit? Satan hates marriage. He is threatened and weakened when we make real commitments. *"Where there is no prophetic vision, there is no restraint, the people dwell carelessly."*[101] We must know that when He the Holy Spirit comes, He will convince us (settle it in our heart). He will convict us, and then bring us to repentance and confirm us with the seal of sonship, so that we cry, "Abba, Father." [102]

It is always the curse of uncertainty that brings the death of authority. We must make our choice today. The Spirit of grace is coming to His church. God is calling for realignment with His plan. He is leading us to rediscover the script that He has written for us to perform on this world's

---

[99] From Daniel 11:32-35
[100] Luke 22:31-34
[101] Proverbs 29:17
[102] John 16:8, Romans 8:15

stage. The Lord is calling us back to the simplicity of the Gospel. God is our chooser.[103] We are his "choosees." Let us forsake the "god of open options" and quit halting, staggering and equivocating with this "untoward" generation that doesn't seem to be toward anything. Joshua 24:15 is a stellar word. *"Choose you this day whom you will serve, as for me and my house we will serve the Lord."*

"I call heaven and earth as a witness today against you, that I have set before you life and death, blessings and cursing; therefore choose life, that both you and your descendants may live...for He is your life!"[104]

God is calling you to reassignment. His calling is now in the marketplace[105] and He says, *"Why do you stand here idle all day?"* Here is the epitome of the harvest call. It is the last hour, and the harvest must be brought in. Our Lord is coming to the "marketplace," the place of many options; about 40,000 choices in your great supermarket. He is asking for your allegiance and commitment to join in the greatest harvest of all the ages *now*. We are to be re-aligned, re-assigned, re-formed, and re-ignited by the flame of the Holy Ghost. Only the people who believe will obey. Let it be you and me.

---

[103] John 15:16, Ephesians 1:4, I Corinthians 1:27, II Thessalonians 2:13
[104] Deuteronomy 30:19 {NKJV}
[105] Mathew 20:6

Chapter Sixteen   *Ever Expanding Horizons*

During the 1980's, while America was enjoying the benefits of being under a wise and effective president (Ronald Reagan) our ministry was being blessed by the Lord with increased outreach in the Findlay area. He also opened many new doors of ministry abroad. The original vision the Lord gave me when he ordained me as His "ambassador to the nations" was now compelling me to respond to the call to many new parts of the world. We traveled to Nigeria with a team from our church to minister in Benin City with Benson Idahosa. Benson was a dynamic young preacher in Nigeria who had built a thriving church with thousands of members. Benson told me that he would like to meet us in Haiti soon. Betty and I had been there many times before. We had established a strong rapport with Jack and Betti Snyder who in turn introduced us to key leaders of that nation.

We planned a time for Benson to meet us in Haiti, and we believed it was God's time to do something special in signs and miracles. Betty and I, along with fellow missionaries, Paul and Eleanor Stern from Africa, traveled to Haiti. We arranged for a meeting with the leaders of the island nation, including "Baby Doc," the president, with Pastor Idahosa. When Benson arrived in Port-au-Prince a few days later we had dinner with a number of government officials. From there we proceeded to the main band shell on the palace grounds for a giant rally. Addressing the great gathering, Benson challenged the powers of "Voodoo," and a great number of miracles and healings occurred in quick succession. Instantly some deaf people could hear clearly. Dumb spirits were forced out of others by the power of God. Throughout the crowd shouts and screams of joyful deliverance could be heard. Many precious souls responded to the Gospel message and gave their hearts to the Lord. This was a major turning point in the history of Haiti. The whole of the demonic Haitian Voodoo system was challenged and shaken to its core.

To appreciate this scene fully, you should be aware of Haiti's early history. Throughout the eighteenth century Haiti was a prosperous nation, exporting as many as three hundred ship loads of produce and merchandise to other places. In 1835 Haiti was officially dedicated to Satan, and Voodoo became the official national religion. Since then Haiti has been a place of pervasive darkness, poverty, and demonic oppression. However after the devastating earthquake in Haiti which killed 350,000 people, we were told recently that Voodoo has been officially renounced by Haiti's president, and Jesus Christ is now declared to be the Lord of Haiti! We are happy to be a part of the army of faithful and anointed soldiers of the Cross who have helped invade that land with weapons of love and healing.

The Lord Stirring Our Nest

The call to minister to the nations intensified in my heart. The Lord sent us key ministers in the early 1980s who brought us strong words of confirmation that our ministry as pastors of Hope Temple was soon to change. I was responding to calls to China where a great and effectual door had opened to us through Shiloh's pastors and missionary Dennis Balcombe, their apostle to China. Betty and I also traveled extensively to Australia, New Zealand, Indonesia, China, and many other nations. The Lord was working and confirming His word in numerous and marvelous ways.

I continued to pastor our beloved congregation, but with an increasing desire to fulfill that heavenly vision which included many more nations. I was constrained by the desire to minister to emerging leaders and pastors. I knew our time in Findlay was nearing fulfillment. I cannot describe the inner anguish of my soul trying to come to terms with the thought of leaving after almost twenty-seven years as pastors. During this process I lost about thirty-five pounds in about six months. (I would be happy to lose that much now.) All that time the overwhelming witness that God was preparing us to launch out totally as "Ambassadors of Hope to the Nations" prevailed.

It was in early April of 1985, during days of corporate fasting and prayer, that I received a call from a friend. He introduced me to a young evangelist named John Muncy. I had invited John to come on a Saturday night to give us a preview of what he was going to teach in the Sunday services. He shared his material on the dangers of hard rock music, with an unusual set of slides and recordings of "satanic back-masking" by various contemporary artists. Frankly, I was appalled by what I heard. We thought that our spiritually mature young people had no need for this message, but I decided to ask John to stay over for a Sunday night meeting.

In the meantime I went to my church study and a great burden of prayer came upon me. I actually started travailing in prayer like I was birthing a baby. I groaned and interceded in the Spirit for over an hour. I thought I was alone in my office, but later realized that John Muncy was sitting in the adjacent office waiting for me.

Something broke loose that Saturday night in the heavenlies and my soul was flooded with expectation. I met John later that evening and said, "I want you to preach beginning tomorrow night (Sunday) through Wednesday." I ministered a fresh word from Isaiah chapter 58 in the Sunday morning service with unusual liberty. We could feel the awesome Spirit of God rising with faith in the Hope Temple family. We experienced a great sense of holy expectation.

That Sunday night John opened with a slide presentation depicting the horror of abortion. He spoke passionately about the critical need for God's people to contend for the innocent lives that were perishing in America.[106]

John then followed with a primitive "lo-tech" slide show depicting some hard rock bands and their lyrics. Suddenly the atmosphere was charged with conviction. It was first

---

[106] At this writing fifty-five million lives have been snuffed out through the cruel practice of abortion in the United States since 1973.

manifest in our own youth, whom John had challenged by asking how many of them knew the lyrics of Led Zeppelin, the Grateful Dead, Ozzie Osborne, and some other notorious groups. To my amazement about 75% of our youth raised their hands indicating that they had memorized many of those lyrics.

Then John, in his inimitable slow Kentucky drawl, closed his session with a slide depicting Jesus, disfigured and bleeding on the cross. He simply asked for those who wanted to forsake the devil and live for Jesus to come forward at once. There was a mass movement toward the front.

The altars were filled very quickly and this scene was repeated each night. By Wednesday night the 2,200-seat sanctuary was packed with young people who had come from all over Findlay and from the surrounding towns. We knew that the meeting would have to go on. We simply could not shut down this obvious move of God. Our son Marcus, our youth pastor Gail Sterling, and our daughter Becky were deeply involved. Jim and Sheryl Menke from the Lima New Hope Center were so faithful in helping in this revival.

The crowds increased each night. The county schools were now sending their buses full of teenagers to these meetings. Many of these youth were saved and gloriously delivered from drugs and alcohol. The school officials were astounded at the dramatic changes in so many students. Several of the administrators came to the meetings to see what was having such an impact on their students. God was delivering a multitude of young people from addictive, sensual, and oppressive lifestyles. It was a miracle of divine grace that changed the spiritual climate in our whole Northwest Ohio area.

John Muncy challenged the entire congregation to repent. This of course included many adults, pastors, and youth leaders from various churches who were witnessing phenomenal changes in their students. The word spread and many people were coming by the bus load from at least seven states around us. This was in 1985; long before the

Toronto airport revival, the Pensacola revival, or the spiritual awakening in Lakeland, Florida. None of us had ever seen anything quite like this. I was physically ill from hearing the filthy lyrics and the terrible sounds of demonic voices that John had recorded by playing the records backward, but this was the word that was touching and releasing the hearts of young people.

We saw an average of 150 souls (mostly youth) literally running to the altar each night to accept the Lord. Our altar stretched about ninety-five feet across our platform, and the groups responding were usually four or five deep! Hungry souls came forward repenting, and they were delivered (many from demonic oppression) and born again. Many were filled with the Holy Spirit. These meetings continued every night for about eight weeks. We recorded over 2200 names of those who were radically converted. (I am sure many more are recorded in heaven.)

At that time we also witnessed a tremendous increase in demonic activity, not only in our area, but throughout our state. The archives of a major newspaper reported that witchcraft was becoming more pervasive in several American cities. In nearby Toledo, Ohio, a number of human sacrifices were recorded.[107] Never in our twenty-seven years of ministry in Ohio had we witnessed this magnitude of satanic manifestation.

Surely the gates of hell were challenged and repelled during the Findlay revival, and many victims of Satan's domain were rescued, redeemed, and transformed into totally new creations. Many of these converts were baptized in water and received the baptism in the Holy Spirit. There was a great number of long-play record albums (one young man offered to bring his four thousand records), tapes, posters, witchcraft and drug paraphernalia, and tobacco brought to the altar each night.

---

[107] Toledo was originally built around a Gypsy camp, and is today considered to have the third largest concentration of witchcraft covens, after Los Angeles and Detroit.

One evening we had a great Holy Ghost bonfire to destroy thousands of dollars worth of accumulated demonic items in several barrels behind the church.[108] We were living in a powerful season of divine intervention. A great crowd gathered around the bonfires, and we could actually hear the demons screaming as the records and tapes were burned. Of course, we did have the fire department's approval, and they were on hand to protect our property. This was the young church in action as it was meant to be.

Findlay, Ohio, would never be the same. As I look back I am constantly amazed at what the Lord accomplished. I have never seen anything like it before or since. We saw profound changes in the lives changed by the power of the simple Gospel, which is the power of God unto salvation. Many of these precious souls have since grown into very effective witnesses and preachers of the Gospel and are serving the Lord in various capacities. We also had a home established in Findlay for pregnant girls to save their babies from abortion. This provided a wonderful alternative where their precious babies' lives could be preserved and nurtured. It was also a place of refuge and recovery for the young mothers.

One of the most powerful things we witnessed during this eight week period was the fulfillment of a great number of prophecies that had been given to us over the years. God watches over His word to perform it!

I now felt that it was time to transition from Findlay into the verified call of God as "Ambassadors of Hope" to the nations. Betty and I took a six week sabbatical in the Smokey Mountains, a place that we dearly loved, to seek the divine will of God. We had stopped there on our honeymoon and then we frequently came back with our kids on some of our vacations. During our stay in the "Smokies" we fasted, prayed, and earnestly sought the Lord for His confirmation.

---

[108] Bible students will recall the account in Acts 19 where, after demonic powers were expelled, great conviction fell on the people. They confessed their deeds and brought numerous evil books, magical arts, idols, and evil fetishes to be burned in the sight of all.

We definitely felt that it was His time for us to leave Findlay and focus on our calling as apostolic missionaries. It was very difficult for us, but we kept moving toward our goal of officially resigning as pastors of Hope Temple.

When the time for our final transition came I made a very serious mistake. I released Hope Temple to the oversight of a young businessman who had been in our church body for about seven years. He had made himself available to be very actively involved in the church and was always eager to speak and lead. He was to be a "chairman" of sorts for an interim period of six months until a mature and godly missionary/pastor could finish his African assignment and then move to Findlay to lead the church. The agreement was that we would have the freedom to come as "pastors emeritus" and Hope Temple would be our permanent home church.

Lesson Learned

We had a delightful farewell service on January 10, 1986. A great number of members and friends came to give us a special send-off, confirming us as "Ambassadors of Hope to the Nations" and as pastors emeritus of Hope Temple. We were assured of continued financial and prayer support by our home church.

Hope Temple as a church was not affiliated with any denomination, but we did have a trans-local team of ministers with spiritual oversight who gave us godly advice. We all felt that this man could fill in for the six month period until the pastor could be installed. The Apostle Paul had warned that if you place a novice in a position to spiritually oversee people he would become lifted up with pride. Abraham Lincoln said, "Most men can stand adversity; but if you want to test a man's character, give him power."

Immediately after our departure this trusted brother began to show his true ambitions. He began to systematically dismantle everything we had accomplished by God's great grace in over twenty-seven years of obedient ministry. He was a "Diotrephes" [109] *"who loved the preeminence and refused to receive us."* He coerced the elders and the church members to elect him as the permanent senior pastor. All our efforts to exhort him to relinquish his position and submit to the Holy Spirit were denied. He repeatedly refused any godly counsel. The man became a legalistic tyrant, trying to rule over the people in the name of the Lord. Over the succeeding months the attendance dropped every week as the disheartened and abused sheep scattered. The once great and vibrant local church dwindled to a handful of cowering stragglers. The man continued each week, deluding himself with the notion that any day a great revival would come under his "holiness" ministry and he would again rule over a large congregation.

Our hearts, as a family, went out to the many faithful members of Hope Temple who had given so much of their time, talent and treasures to make this a truly exceptional family of believers. I have grieved and repented over the great mistake that I was fully responsible for, and I have openly asked our precious Hope family for their forgiveness, and they have given it. Thankfully most of the former members have settled into good churches in the area. Some of these churches we had helped to plant and mentor over the years.

One day in March 1989, we received the news that the beautiful sanctuary that we had built adjacent to our first chapel had burned to the ground. The evidence proved that it was arson. We still don't know all the facts, nor was the arsonist named. Only the chapel remained and this man in his vain glory still holds meetings with a handful of people. He removed the sign of Hope Temple immediately after we left, and it is now a "no name" building. The light has gone out. We are still praying for the Lord to "revive His work in the midst of the years" with our Hope Temple family.

---

[109] III John vs. 9

Chapter Seventeen

Ambassadors of Hope at

Large

Betty and I found solace in moving into a little condominium in Columbus, Ohio. Our son, Marcus, moved in with us, as he was working with Pastor Rod Parsley. He was helping him design the World Harvest Outreach Center, especially focusing on the television studios and technical installations. We were still living close enough to most of our family in Findlay, and we were blessed to be received with honor by Pastor Rod Parsley at the World Harvest Church. I was asked to minister there on several occasions and we witnessed the Lord's blessing on that great group of believers.

Our dear friends, Daryl and Barb Sanders, who had been part of our body in Hope Temple, teamed up with Dean and Patty Demos to plant Zion Church, located on the north side of Columbus. We were honored to also be a small part of this wonderful body of believers during our time living in Columbus. From there we continued to travel abroad to many countries, fulfilling our mandate to preach the Gospel to the nations.

A Mighty Prayer Revival

During my travels I met Pastor Larry Lea in Van Nuys, California, at a special meeting with Dr. Jack Hayford. Larry had heard about our revival and the worship symposiums that were now well-known in many places. Larry asked me to come to Rockwall, Texas, to be a spiritual father and elder at the great Church on the Rock. Larry led early-morning prayer sessions daily with so many attending that the state police had to direct traffic. The church was growing exponentially, and we felt a real witness to move to Rockwall, Texas. That was a very significant move because the Lord connected us with so many precious folks like Les and Julia Horvath, Les (junior) and Gloria Horvath, Ron and Judy Minth, David and Naomi Shibley, Bob and Velma Wilhite,

Lawrence and Coral Kennedy, and many others who became lifelong friends.

We had a beautiful home built right near Lake Hubbard in Rockwall. Betty made it just adorable on the inside and I worked on the landscape outside with God sent helpers. Marcus and Michael our sons were also living nearby. Our family situation was ideal.

During these days I traveled extensively among the Church on the Rock satellite church ministries. I also traveled overseas teaching and mentoring church leaders in Africa, India (with David Shibley, Bob Wichita, Mel Cooley, and others), Europe, and China.

The Crumbling Walls of Communism

At that time we were watching the literal dismantling of the communist system in the Soviet Union. During those exciting days[110] we heard of the demise of Ceausescu, the President of Romania, and the subsequent riots in Timisoara, Romania. We had been traveling in many of these countries over the years, but always with heavy interference from the communist leaders. On a special trip with Jan Barendse from Holland, we entered into East Germany where we witnessed the dissolving of the Soviet border security. It was an exciting moment when we entered the border control near Erfort, East Germany. We had experienced great difficulty in getting through that checkpoint with all of our Bibles and equipment, but about three days later [111] we returned through that same border, and there was no security at all! The Stazi (border guards) had all gone and the border was wide open. I remember how thrilled I was to drive into Berlin and help knock down the Berlin wall with a sledge hammer. God was truly at work. This was not the work of any government, nor was a shot fired by any nation. God sovereignly confounded and

---

[110] Christmas day, 1989

[111] after a glorious meeting, including visiting Luther's Seminary and getting to sleep in Martin Luther's bed!

brought down the Soviet Union. He is the same God who can deal with Islam!

Budapest Bound

It was in the fall of 1990, when I had just returned home from one of my ministry trips to Hungary, Germany, and Romania, when I learned that our son Marcus and his mother had been strategizing. Marcus said, "Dad maybe it is time for you and Mom to move to Hungary. They need your ministry there more that they do here in America." I looked at Betty, and she was smiling and nodding her approval. I thought, why should I pray anymore? This has to be God, because Betty had frequently asked me to never take her back to Hungary again. [112]

I did pray and seek confirmation and counsel. We all felt Hungary would be receptive to apostolic ministry, and I was especially qualified to preach there because I spoke the language. I had an immediate peace in my heart that this was God reordering our steps. We came into agreement with all of our children, and then proceeded to sell our beautiful home in Rockwall, Texas.

There was just one problem. The real estate market had "bottomed out." There were beautiful new homes on our street that were selling for less than we had to have out of our place. We prayed.

Then the Lord spoke to me and said, "Whose house is it anyway?"

"Your's, Lord."

"Put up a sign that says, 'By Owner,' and see what happens."

I found a "By Owner" sign in a friend's garage. After I changed the phone number on it, I took my hammer and pounded it down in front of our house. By the time I had walked back around the house to put my hammer in the garage the front door bell was ringing.

---

[112] It was under the Communist regime when she visited there a few years before, and it was not very welcoming.

An apparently excited lady was standing there. She said, "I just drove in from California, and I am looking for a home to buy. This is the first place that I saw with a for sale sign out front."

Betty replied, "Come back tomorrow. We're having an open house."

"No, I must see it today!"

She and her husband came, and they both loved the house. They paid the asking price, and then bought most of our furniture as well.

Our dear friends in the Church on the Rock gave us a wonderful send-off, laying hands on us and commending us to our new venture as "Ambassadors of Hope to Hungary." Our sons, Tom and Marcus, helped us print up some brochures that carried the endorsements of several key leaders in the Body of Christ. The rest of our kids helped us load our container for the journey to Hungary.

We arrived in Budapest with a large shipping container. It held our Ford van, our furniture, and supplies. The Word of the Lord specifically to me was from Jeremiah 29:7. He told us to pray for *"the peace of the city where he had taken us, and in the peace of this city we would have peace and prosperity."* We set about to love, teach, and mentor many emerging leaders. God also gave us favor with the older saints as well.

Budapest, Hungary
Parliament on the Danube River

After looking around the city for a home we rented a flat on the third floor of a large house. The owners had two large dogs to intimidate us, but we still felt secure. God gave us a gracious entrance into the hearts of the Hungarian people. The language that Grandma had taught me came back easily to my mind. I was soon teaching, preaching, and even translating in Hungarian.

We lived in Budapest for about four years. The Lord gave us the privilege of traveling all over Hungary, preaching in cities, towns and villages. We were not only preaching the Gospel, but at the same time we were building bridges between different denominational and cultural groups in that nation.

At this time the Lord opened the door for us to travel into the Soviet Union, especially into Moscow, where we ministered to over 1000 students at a time in the great Olympic Izmialova Hotel. Our friend Bob Wiener was the leader of this awesome movement in the universities. Several others from the United States joined us in that ministry, including David Kiteley, Daryl Sanders, and Bart Pierce.

This was an unprecedented time when young people could fly round-trip from anywhere in the eleven time zones of the vast Soviet Union to Moscow for $3.00 in U.S. dollars. We were able to arrange for each student to stay for five days at the Olympic Izmialovo Hotel for $2.00 per day, and that included the room and meals.

The doors for ministry were wide open. It was exhilarating to see how hungry these folks were for the Gospel that had been so bitterly repressed by their Marxist rulers for over seventy-five years. I was there when the tanks were still firing at the "White House," the presidential palace, and the parliament buildings. Gorbachev was in hiding. Buses were burning in the streets. No one seemed to know who was in charge.

Boris Yeltsin

One day Bill Gothard, a renowned Bible teacher with a great national youth ministry in America,[113] called me in Budapest. He asked me to arrange for a major purchase of wheat to be shipped from Hungary to Moscow. Bill was training hundreds of Russian young people for ministry in their own country. The Lord gave me favor with the Hungarian government, and I arranged to have fifty-three railroad cars loaded with wheat and shipped to Moscow. It was fun standing in the rail yard and giving the signal to the engineer to start rolling toward the Russian border. There was an armed contingent of Russian soldiers that would guard the train until it arrived at its destination.

Bill Gothard then asked me to come to Moscow and help teach his young students. While I was there Bill received a call from President Boris Yeltsin who had established himself as the titular head of the disintegrating Soviet Union. He had to get away from his meeting with the heads of the fast dissolving former Soviet Union, who were meeting at the Kremlin. Mr. Yeltsin proposed a meeting with us at the International Tennis Match that was taking place in the prestigious Moscow Sports Stadium.

Bill and I were driven in the official Kremlin limousine and led up to the "presidential box" where Mrs. Yeltsin was already there waiting for us. Soon the President and his entourage of body guards and officials arrived. Through our interpreters we were able to share the Gospel with Mr. and Mrs. Yeltsin. He then asked us to especially pray for him and his country for their success, and for recovery from the malaise of the past years. It was a thrilling and historic moment as we prayed for the Yeltsin's.

It was amazing to see the wonderful ways the Lord gave us favor to be in strategic places where history was being made. From our vantage point in Budapest we witnessed the total dissolving of the political union of the fifteen Soviet

---

[113] The ministry is now called "Institute in Basic Life Principles," headquartered in Oakbrook, Illinois.

states. Although the governments of the individual nations are still largely communist in their methods and ideology, the freedom for missionaries and church planters has resulted in tremendous growth in the Kingdom of God in that part of the world.

While I was preaching to the students at one of our frequent meetings in the Izmailovo Hotel, the Lord gave me a prophetic word about Kiev. I said, "This capital city of Ukraine shall become the 'Antioch' of Russia." About seventy young people in the audience who had traveled there from Kiev shouted for joy! It was only later that I learned that Kiev was indeed the very place were Andrew the Apostle was sent to preach the Gospel to the heathen in Russia during the first century. Later, in about 1000 A.D., the grandmother of Crown Prince Vladimir was visiting in Constantinople, Turkey. She was converted to Christianity by the orthodox priests there. They charged her to go home and spread the news of the Gospel to her idol-worshipping nation. She told the Turkish bishops that her grandson, the crown prince, was almost blind with an eye ailment. They anointed her hands with oil and commissioned her to anoint her grandson with oil and believe God to heal him.

When she arrived back in Kiev, her grandson was very attentive to her message. He said, "If Jesus Christ will heal my eyes, I will be converted, and I will command our whole nation to be baptized also." God healed him, and history records that multitudes were baptized in one day as they flung their great wooden idols into the Dniepper River.[114] The Gospel subsequently spread to all of the "Russes," the Russian states, and finally into Moscow. The Kremlin was then built to house the Orthodox Churches and protect them from the heathen marauders of that time. The time had come for God to revive his work in Kiev.

---

[114] This scene is beautifully preserved on a twelve-foot long tapestry in the Russian Orthodox Church in Philadelphia, Pennsylvania.

Kiev: the Antioch of Russia

In the late fall of 1991, from our home in Budapest, Betty and I were asked to make arrangements for James and Betty Robison and their staff, including our son Marcus, to travel to Kiev.[115] James Robison Ministries had responded to the Chernobyl nuclear explosion. They brought relief to many of the victims, and especially ministered to hundreds of children in the Number Fourteen Children's Hospital in Kiev.

I made arrangements with my Hungarian friend, who owned a flight charter service, to fly the James Robison team to Kiev. Betty and I did not fit on that flight because they had so much equipment and so many supplies with them. The Lord arranged for our own private Aeroflot Jet. It was a 150-passenger TU-154 that had secretly flown Jewish refugees into Hungary that day and was returning "empty" to Kiev. We had friends in the Aeroflot office in Budapest (and friends in high places) that whisked us onto that plane. There was a total of two passengers and nine crew members aboard. We actually arrived in Kiev before the James Robinson crew! The pilots were former Mig fighter pilots who graciously allowed me to fly "third seat" with them. They landed with such force that all the seat backs fell forward. What a ride!

God gave us so much favor in those days with the free flights and with great cargos of supplies to help the Chernobyl Children's Hospital in Kiev. It was a pleasure to serve with James and Betty Robison who helped immensely in bringing in the needed supplies. Jan Barense, a faithful minister companion for many years, was our facilitator. He also brought in many truck loads of goods from Holland. Those were truly miraculous days for us and for the Ukraine. God opened to us a great and glorious door of hope to that important part of the former Soviet Union.

---

[115] Marcus was working for James Robison Ministries at that time as their television broadcast director.

Divine Connections

One day, in March, 1992, I met in Moscow with our dear friends Daryl and Barb Sanders and their friend Dr. Donald Quick, from the M. D. Anderson Hospital in Houston, Texas. They were bringing special blood analyzing equipment and medical supplies for our project in Kiev's Number Fourteen Children's Hospital. We were scheduled to fly from Moscow to Kiev. Our bags were checked and we waited patiently for the fuel truck to arrive with fuel for the Aeroflot TU-154 Tri-motor jet. We had rented a large bus and hired a driver for a total of eight dollars for the day. He was to drive us wherever we wanted to go in Moscow. As we unloaded our bags at the airport I had a very keen sense that we were not to let the driver leave with the bus. He agreed to stay until we were on the plane and in the air.

After many hours of delay, we were finally told that the flight was cancelled. Our only recourse was to take the train, a fourteen-hour ride. We joyfully thanked God to see that our bus and driver were still there. We loaded our bags back on board and directed our driver to take us to the train station. In the meantime a well-dressed man, standing with his wife and bodyguard, was knocking on our bus door and asking to come aboard. We later learned that this was an important man who was also scheduled to fly on the same flight to Kiev. He was the president of the World Bank for Eastern Europe, out of Washington, D.C. He told us that his private jet had landed in Moscow, but it did not have enough fuel to carry him to Kiev. "Could we please ride along with you?" After we stopped at the Pizza Hut, we purchased their tickets also. We boarded the train after our bus driver bribed the ticket agent to get us on board.[116] Amazingly, Daryl, Barb, Don, and I were given a "state" cabin with four bunks, while our friend the bank president had to separate from his wife and bodyguard. They each had to sleep in separate rooms, sharing a spare bunk here and there with various families. We spent the whole night talking with our friend

---

[116] The cost was an extra $1.50.

about Jesus, and enjoying the "deli" food basket I had brought from Hungary.

We finally arrived after fourteen hours on the train. We had a very warm reception at our Kiev children's hospital.[117] We delivered our medical supplies and had a very good meeting with the chief surgeon and his staff. They soon became like family to us. This was a trip that was to open a great door of opportunity for us to bring the Gospel of hope to so many suffering families. We enjoyed "loving on" and praying with the sick children. We also delighted in bringing gifts and hope to them.

When we finished our visit at the hospital we looked for the driver who had been assigned to us. He was supposed to wait for us outside the hospital. When we stepped out into the parking lot we saw that he was gone. We realized that we were stranded. There was no taxi service, and we had no way of knowing what trolley to take back to our hotel in the city, so we prayed. Just as we finished our prayer a tall, distinguished-looking black man appeared. I spoke to him and said, "Sir, do you speak English?"

"Yes sir."

"Do you speak Ukrainian?"

"Yes sir."

"Well, my name is Moses." I shook his hand.

"My name is Seraphim!" he exclaimed. "I am here to serve you."

God had sent a black angel to guide us. He was a doctor from Africa. He had received his medical training there in Kiev. He took charge and flagged down a car. He ordered the driver to take us all back to our hotel. We enjoyed a good dinner. Somehow our benefactor slipped away, and we never saw him again.

God's word does not return void. I had prophesied that the next great revival would start in Kiev some days before. We actually watched as the whole drama played out before

---

[117] The 1200 beds were dedicated to the children who were victims of the Chernobyl nuclear disaster.

our eyes. A young man from Siberia, who had been led to the Lord through a good friend of mine, met us and became our guide. I rented the Yellow Palace Opera House for one hundred dollars (U.S.) for a one-night evangelistic meeting with our minister friends from America, including Violet Kiteley, David Kiteley, Daryl Sanders, Bart Pierce, and Ann Gimenez.

Maurud, our young "troubadour," led us through the main square in Kiev.[118] As he strummed his guitar, curious folks by the score asked us, "Where did you come from, and what are you doing in Kiev?" We invited them all to join us at the Yellow Palace Opera house at 6:00. At that point we still needed an interpreter. I finally met a student in the square who was from Zambia. His name was Henry Moldava.

"Do you know Jesus?"

"Yes."

"Can you speak English?

"Yes, and I speak Ukrainian also."

I conscripted him on the spot to be our interpreter for the meeting that night. Henry agreed and he proved to be a fine interpreter.

What a glorious night it turned out to be. The auditorium was filled, simply by word of mouth "advertising," and the sovereign presence of the Holy Spirit filled the house. Henry was anointed as he interpreted for each of us. When the altar call was given the response was beyond our imagination. About 90% of all the hundreds of people attending voiced a prayer to accept Jesus Christ as the Lord of their lives, and many more came forward to receive the Baptism in the Holy Spirit.

We then worked with Bart Pierce and John and Ann Gimenez from the Rock Churches of Baltimore and Virginia Beach, to help establish a local church. The Lord gave us favor with officials and we were able to lease the great Lenin Museum, which was located on the main square. It was a beautiful building that housed a sixty-foot tall basalt statue

---

[118] At the time workers were dismantling a gigantic monument to Lenin.

of Lenin. There was a large auditorium underneath where official state guests had been entertained during the years of the Soviet Union. God's favor was everywhere. The manager did not want cash, but asked me to give her some spare video equipment we had in exchange for a one year lease! This was the beginning of a mighty revival that sprang out of the soil of what was the epicenter of a revival in Kiev one thousand years before.

Since that beginning revival God has blessed Henry Moldava. He now leads a great congregation in Kiev, numbering several thousand. In more recent years another African, Pastor Sunday Adelaja from Nigeria, has led a congregation of about forty thousand in Kiev. It is the largest church in the Ukraine. God's Word does not return void. God watches over His Word to perform it.

Betty and I made many trips back to Kiev from our headquarters in Budapest. The Lord gave us favor with the managers and directors of Aeroflot Russian Airlines, and also with the Hungarian Malev Airlines. We were given free passes to fly, and also to transport many tons of supplies into Kiev, free of charge. Our first Easter in the Soviet Union was so amazing, as we saw great banners stretched over the main streets in Russian proclaiming "He is risen." Hallelujah! The Word of God was springing forth, and it would bring forth a mighty harvest that still continues all over the former Soviet Union.

One morning while we were in our apartment in Budapest, the Lord awakened me early with a word in my ear. He said, "Ask of me, and I will give you the heathen for your inheritance, and the uttermost parts of the earth for your possession."[119] I said, "Lord, who do you want me to ask for?" He responded, "Ask me for Cuba, and ask me for Castro." A great burden came over me to pray for Cuba, and especially for Fidel Castro, the communist dictator of Cuba at the time. I have visited Cuba twice since then, and I am still praying for Cuba and Castro.

---

[119] Psalm 2: 8

162

During our extensive stay in Budapest, Hungary, we could travel by car to as many as seven countries in one day. The Lord gave us favor with many emerging Christian leaders and new churches were springing up, including many Gypsy congregations. These folks were really on fire for God, and a good number of them were great musicians. We had the joy of entertaining many groups from abroad.

All of this time I was meeting with and mentoring leaders in the Hungarian churches. The Kingdom of God was flourishing throughout Eastern Europe despite the efforts of the Marxist rulers to suppress and even destroy Christianity throughout the preceding seventy-five years. We witnessed the actual disintegration of atheistic communism. In Budapest, Hungary, we fervently prayed several times a week with a faithful group of intercessors right in the Parliament building cabinet rooms. We also met with Victor Orban, the president of Hungary, on several occasions. The Lord granted us favor with many of the top political leaders of Hungary and with numerous spiritual leaders as well. God had answered our prayers. The Hungarian Parliament passed a law that all school children through the seventh grade had to have Bible instruction. The Lord gave me specific instructions when we arrived in Budapest.

> *"Seek (inquire for, require, and request) the peace and welfare of the city to which I have caused you to be carried away captive; and pray for it, for in the welfare of (the city in which you live) you will have peace (welfare)."*[120]

Wonderful doors of opportunity kept opening wider in Hungary. God then added another source of great blessing and strength. Our close friends, Paul and Eleanor Stern, who were living in Germany at the time, moved in with us in Budapest. They introduced us to David and Mary Clark, veteran missionaries they knew from the time they spent serving God in Africa. David told us that he was instructed by God to go into Uzgharod, Moldovia, and preach the

---

[120] Jeremiah 29:7

Gospel on the streets. It was in this area that the Soviet army had its largest tank battalion training grounds, as well as its top-secret jet fighter squadron. Two well-dressed men who had heard David preach there on the street approached him and asked if they could meet him for coffee. They said, "We have heard your message. We want you to come to our secret base and bring this message of hope to our officers in training."

David Clark agreed and arranged for us to travel with him to that military base. Our dear friends from Canada, Baldwin and Lucy Verstraete, and another brother from Beaumont, Texas, came along with us. We loaded our little Dodge van with many Bibles, tracts, and supplies, and headed for the border. God sovereignly favored us. Somehow we were allowed to go to the head of a long line of vehicles that had been stalled there for three days. We had to supply the paper for our visas, and of course a pound of coffee and some chocolates. We thought we should be gracious and leave little tips for the border police.

Russian officers receive the Gospel at Uzgharod, Moldovia, 1992

We were thrilled with godly expectation as we arrived at the Uzgharod Military Base auditorium. Many hundreds of airmen and officers were dressed in their best uniforms and sitting in order, ready to receive the Gospel. After we shared the Word of the Lord the response was like thunder! They unanimously declared out loud, "Yes! I want Jesus Christ to be my Lord and Savior!" We prayed with many of them and gave Bibles to all that came. This was the beginning of an ongoing ministry that David and Mary Clark carried on until the Lord called David home. Our Texas brother, Robert, returned to that area and planted several churches that are still thriving in Moldovia and Ukraine. God is so faithful.

Many volumes could be written about our adventures while stationed in Hungary. Our home in Budapest became a little Grand Central Station for many visitors from abroad. James and Betty Robinson, John and Ann Gimenez, James and Ann Beall, Jerry Kaufman, Paul and Eleanor Stern, Frank and Ruth Muncey, Phil Stern, David and Marilyn Kiteley, Moses and Trudy Lendenhour, our own family members, and many others made our home their Hungarian haven.

We also had a delegation of twenty young people, led by Liane Verstraete, from Evangel Temple in Toronto. We traveled with them in our friend's chartered bus into Romania and Ukraine. Together we visited the Kiev Hospital, and enjoyed preaching and singing to many churches throughout Eastern Europe. Many precious souls were changed by the power of the Gospel.

Dean Demos, after serving as our music director at Hope Temple, became the chief musician for Christ for the Nations in Dallas. While teaching and directing music there he led a large group of singers and musicians to Hungary to minister among us. What a great blessing they were! We traveled with these groups into Romania, Bulgaria, Austria, Germany, and many parts of the former Soviet Union. The Lord worked mightily through us and confirmed His word with many amazing miracles.

Chapter Eighteen

Homeward Bound

After many fulfilling adventures abroad, during the summer of 1993, we felt that the Lord would have us come home to America. We decided to settle in Clearwater Florida, where we were received warmly by Pastor John Lloyd and the wonderful congregation of Clearwater Christian Center. While there we continued to travel extensively and minister to many leaders and emerging shepherds in many new countries.

It was a special treat to have our entire family gather in Palm Springs, California, to help us celebrate our fortieth wedding anniversary on August 29, 1993.

The Call to Cuba

In the spring of 1994, my close friend and prayer partner, Lyle Bertsch, traveled with me and Danny Alexander of Florida, to Cuba. We were joined with Franco Genarro, a missionary friend who had relatives in Cuba and had ministered there previously. The Lord gave us great favor and we witnessed many wonderful meetings in Cuba, including preaching at the Central Methodist Cathedral with Bishop Romero. Pastor Alejandro was also a great blessing, and we enjoyed coming to his church. Several years later I returned to Cuba with Robi Evans from Morelia, Mexico, for pastors' conferences in several cities. Cuba is still on my heart, and I hope to return there soon. Fresh fires of revival are now burning in that communist-ruled island nation, and the people are definitely more open to the Gospel than ever before!

A New Home

In 1995 we were again directed by the Lord to move to California. Most of our family, including four of our children and their offspring, were living and working in southern California. We felt that it was time to settle in San Clemente. The Lord so graciously provided us with a beautiful new home near the ocean, and we have enjoyed living here for the past seventeen years. Family is the most important part of our lives. Our large and growing family is our legacy and our heritage.

In San Clemente we were welcomed into Life Church by Pastors Phil and Jeannie Munsey. For many years I have had the privilege of teaching foundation classes and sharing the Word periodically with this precious family of believers. During this time I continued to travel and to help teach and mentor emerging pastors and leaders in many countries.

Ethiopia Reaches Out

In Psalm 68:31 the Psalmist in his prophetic song declared, *"Ethiopia shall soon stretch out her hands unto God."* At different intervals during the years 1994 to 1997 we joined Pastor David Kiteley and his team in Addis Ababa to meet with hundreds of key evangelical leaders. At one time we had a major prophetic conference in Debre-Zeit, Ethiopia. Gary Munson and Violet Kiteley had blazed the trail before us. They had encouraged the evangelical pastors who had just been liberated from the tyrannical communist rule that had prevailed for many years.

God ordained a unique variety of meetings in Ethiopia where we had the privilege of sharing on the fullness of God's plan in the restoration of all the gifts of the Spirit, as well as the gifted five-fold ministry. Hundreds of these dedicated brethren have responded to the Word of the Lord, and we had the pleasure of ministering to them by the laying on of hands and prophecy. There has been a tremendous breakthrough in the evangelical community and throughout the nation. Subsequently we have been making ministry trips to Ethiopia over the years, and the Lord has added mightily to the building of His Kingdom there. Many denominational leaders have come together in one accord. The government provided a large piece of land for the building of Shiloh Bible College in Hawassa. Dr. Gary Munson was sent forth from Shiloh Church in Oakland. He moved to Ethiopia with his family and established a beautiful home there. He then presided over the building of Shiloh Bible College which has been wonderfully successful in training vibrant spiritual leaders.

It is a great joy to report that the Word of God has prevailed, and now Gary Munson heads up eight Bible schools where multiplied hundreds of leaders have been trained over the past two decades. Most of these leaders were sovereignly rescued out of Islam by a direct personal confrontation with Jesus. In fact in one year over 110 former Imams[121] graduated from the Shiloh Bible Colleges and joined many others who are now planting hundreds of churches throughout the country. Some of these dedicated brethren are reaching into surrounding African countries with the Gospel with dramatic results. Ethiopia has stretched out her hands to God, and God has taken hold of their hands in a mighty awakening that is affecting the destiny of multitudes.

There is a fresh wind blowing in Ethiopia. On a recent trip, we took a team of worshippers and ministers to Awassa in response to an invitation from the Christian students at the Awassa University. This great campus of eighteen thousand students is directly across the road from our Shiloh Bible School campus. The Lord gave us great favor, and over 3,000 young Christian worshippers gathered to lift their voices in unison and rededicate their lives to reaching their nation for Christ. From Ethiopia we traveled to Kenya to minister in prophetic presbytery with Pastor Don Matheny

---

[121] Muslim clerics, something like Islamic "pastors"

and his wonderful family and church in the Nairobi Lighthouse.

Our team consisted of John Stevenson, his drummer Eddie Lucky (from Cincinnati), Gary Munson, and Pastor David Frech (from Church of the Harvest, Kansas City, Missouri). David Frech is one of our spiritual sons from our ministry at Hope Temple. The Lord has given us many spiritual sons and daughters over the years in many countries. Many of them call me "Papa Moses," and Betty is known as "Grandma Moses."

Purpose Driven

Our beloved son Marcus was very instrumental in helping Rick Warren in his development of a DVD format for his book, *The Purpose Driven Church*. Marcus helped get it translated and recorded in many languages, including Hungarian. In November of 1999, after a few years of living in Southern California, Betty and I were called back to Budapest, Hungary, for another season of ministry as special Ambassadors of Hope with the Purpose Driven Church curriculum with a DVD format to teach emerging Hungarian leaders and pastors. Many churches were edified and encouraged.

Encounters of a Heavenly Kind

I went on ahead to Hungary to secure an apartment for us. I packed my bags and headed for the Orange County Airport to fly to Holland and then on to Hungary. I felt a strange uneasiness, actually a nostalgic loneliness, as Betty drove me to the airport. I was usually very up-beat when getting ready to board a flight. But this morning I was feeling down, and actually having a pity party. I thought of all the people we had prophesied over, in so many countries over the course of so many years. Here I was going on this trip, leaving my wife at the airport, and no one had prophesied or encouraged me. The cloud over me could be felt.

As I boarded the plane the flight attendant looked at me and exclaimed, "There you are, you mighty man of God!

You're the guy who kept me praying early this morning. You have said that you wanted to hear a word from God. Well, you're going to hear that word. Now, where are you sitting?"

I was shaking as I handed her the ticket. "Good!" she said. "You are first class.[122] God had told me that if you boarded with a coach ticket I was to bring you up here to first class.[123] Now be seated, and I will come and give you the word of the Lord after we level off in flight."

By then I was really shaking. Soon Susie Diehl came and knelt by my seat and began to pour out a powerful prophetic word confirming our move to Budapest and all that the Lord would do there. I was thinking, "Why don't I have a tape recorder?" Susie spoke up and said, "Don't worry about the tape recorder. I will write down everything God has to say to you," and she did. I had witnessed to a large number of flight attendants on many of my trips, but I never had one prophesy to me. God is so faithful. He watches over His word to perform it.

Betty soon joined me again in Budapest, and we gathered a very dedicated group of over one hundred pastors and leaders. We were blessed to have the use of the old Scottish Presbyterian Church where I taught Rick Warren's Purpose Driven Church curriculum for about sixteen weeks.

The Lord has been gracious to give us favor and friendship with so many Spirit-anointed ministers. We are eternally grateful for His grace and provision. Our friends John and Wendy Beckett of Elyria, Ohio, (who have supported us so faithfully over the years) visited us during that time. We had John share a powerful word on *Loving Monday*, from a book he had written, to a large gathering of business leaders we hosted in a prominent hotel on the Danube River in Budapest. These were significant and glorious days for Hungary and for many emerging leaders that we had the privilege of training.

---

[122] Someone had given me an upgraded ticket.
[123] I wish that more flight attendants were that sensitive.

Chapter Nineteen   *Instant in Season*

My Lord has been my "nurse,"[124] my "mentor," and my "guide."[125] He made my mouth as His mouth.[126] So many times the word of the Lord came through my lips and I was totally amazed at what He had said through me. Our God is faithful, and He watches over His word to perform it. God is not giving us the silent treatment. He has wired each one of his children for sound. I have discovered that it is God's purpose to make His church a prophetic community. We are to speak as the "oracles of God." [127]

Allow me to illustrate just how this works. One day as my friend Mike Hanchett and I were leaving a business leaders' prayer meeting in San Juan, California, we encountered a man coming up the stairs. I noticed that he was carrying a political sign. As I stepped down on his level, I suddenly spoke out, "Hey! What is it that you want me to pray about for you today?" He was shocked, and so was I!

"Who the (expletives) are you?"

"I am Moses."

"Don't put me on."

I handed him my card, and he was shocked to see the Vegh name.

"Are you related to Tom Vegh?"

"Yes, sir. Tom is my son."

He then handed me his card. I then learned that he had been Tom's commanding general at the El Torro base of the Marine Corps, F-4 Squadron, where Tom had trained as a fighter pilot. He suddenly changed his demeanor, and said, "Please go down to that car parked at the curb and pray for my wife. She was just released from the hospital. Mike and I went down and she immediately responded and said, "Yes, I

---

124 Psalm 139
125 Psalm 32:8-10
126 Jeremiah 15:19
127 1 Peter 4.10

need healing, but we also need a miraculous answer about a court case that is pending."

We prayed, and a few days later I received a call saying we must meet. I met the general, and he presented me with a beautiful card of thanks from his wife. She had been healed, and that very day God answered our prayer for a favorable court decision! I have had many exciting encounters just following Jesus, who goes about healing all that are oppressed by the devil.[128]

A Glorious Encounter

Many have asked me over the years how it is that I just keep going and answering the call to many countries; ministering in settings ranging from large cities to the most inaccessible and remote places in the world. By God's grace I have stood on six continents (and nearly seven). I preached the glorious Gospel of His Kingdom in Invacargo, New Zealand, which is the departure point to the Antarctic (the seventh continent).

It was in the summer of 2004 that Betty and I had the privilege to minister in Kuala, Lumpur, with our good friend Henry Pillai of Grace Assembly. I preached in both of their large assemblies that morning. Pastor Henry then asked Betty and me to join him for lunch. We were to be the guests of a very special family. Our host was Chau Juimeng, a high-ranking government official who was later to run for a seat in the Parliament of Malaysia. His wife, Honey, and their family all greeted us in their family restaurant. It was a sumptuous meal and we had a beautiful time together. After our twelve course dinner Chua Jiumeng pounded his fists on the table and shouted, "I want the Holy Ghost!"

"When?"

He said, "Now!"

Henry and I laid hands upon him and suddenly he burst out, speaking in a heavenly language. His wife, children, and

---

[128] Acts 10:38 & 1 John 3:8

all his guests were filled with the Holy Spirit with the evidence of speaking in other tongues.

The Veghs with the Chua Family

Shortly after that I received a letter from their son Damien (who was among those who had been filled with the Spirit at that time). I felt constrained to write him back and tell him to print out Psalm ninety-one and post it where he could read it daily and memorize it. About three months later I received a tremendous testimony from Damien. He told of being kidnapped by two bandits who car-jacked him. Their plan was to rob him, take him to his bank at knife point, steal his money and his car, and then kill him. As they were driving, he was quoting Psalm ninety-one. They were caught in a "round about" traffic circle. A stranger walked up to the car and jerked the driver's door open, demanding that he get out. The bandit then shoved the car in gear and found an opening that led him down another road, all the while looking in his rear view mirror. The police saw him driving erratically and set up a road block where he crashed. The thieves were arrested, and Damien was set free. Then the thief told about the giant "angel" (three meters tall) that had opened his door and pursued him as he traveled at high speeds. This guy was glad to be caught. The robbery was foiled, all the suspects were caught, and Damien's testimony was published in the main newspapers of Malaysia about his "Psalm ninety-one deliverance." God does give his angels charge over you! The Chua family has been a tremendous blessing to me in my travels to Asia, always providing a "prophet's chamber" and great fellowship.

About ten years ago the Lord also brought me into contact with Vela Tan, a man who loves the Lord and has been a very dedicated church planter as the owner of large palm oil plantations in Borneo and Malaysia. I have been honored to minister for Vela on several occasions, dedicating at least three of the churches he started. So far he has pioneered fourteen churches throughout Sandakan. He and his wife Jamint, along with his brothers K. H. and Saygin and their families, are like our family in Sandakan. Their hospitality and fellowship remind me of the relationship Onesiphorus had with the Apostle Paul.[129]

Serendipity in New Mexico

One of my most rewarding trips was to a precious group of believers in Fort Sumner, New Mexico. Anna Teeter, who had just recently lost her husband, was the pastor. The Church was called simply, the "Church on the Hill," and to me the area was like the end of the world. I found the quaint little former military outpost about three hours from the Albuquerque airport. It was there that the notorious "Billy the Kid" was killed. This town had one grocery store, a post-office, and one drug store with an old fashioned soda fountain where we were treated each evening to a luscious milk shake. There was also one motel, and I had a room in it. I counted many of the ninety-six freight trains coming by my room each day. I was actually offered a "saddled quarter horse" to be stationed at my motel just in case I wanted to go somewhere. I opted for the pickup and driver.

I was honored by these dear saints to minister at their annual missions convention where some of the people had driven up to 700 miles to be there. This gracious family of

---

[129] II Timothy 1:16

believers showered me with so much love that I accepted their invitation to return with great joy. I discovered my destiny had pathways already marked out.

Revival Fires in the Congo

Another notable divine encounter the Lord had ordained was our trip to Kenya with our friends Paul and Eleanor Stern. Betty remained in Nairobi with Eleanor at the King's Kids Orphanage that the Sterns had built. Paul and I boarded a beautiful new Pilatus plane, a missionary assistance flight (MAF) to Bukavu in the Congo. We arrived

at our destination in less than two hours. The supply trucks and equipment traveled on Kenya's not-so-well-maintained roads, and it took them sixteen days to make the same trip. Here we joined forces with Roger and Shireen West. Their ministry is called "Revival Fires." They had worked with

Betty and Moses with a Massai tribesman in Kenya

Rhinehardt Bonke for several years in great African crusades. Roger and Shireen are God's anointed evangelists to the Congo and to many other countries as well.

We were hosted in the old Swedish mission in Bukavu and graciously served by dedicated missionaries, including fearless Charlene Harris. She had often traveled alone in her Suzuki jeep many hundreds of miles through the jungles, inhabited by many warring tribes, to carry the Gospel to Bukavu. She was tireless as a faithful servant of the Lord to go wherever He sent her.

Evangelistic meetings were conducted on the soccer field every day, and we watched as the mighty power of the Holy Spirit delivered many thousands from sin and sickness. Many of the people also received the baptism in the Holy

Spirit. On the last night of the crusade about 94,000 people jammed into the field. They stood for hours in the copious rain showers, and the Lord Jesus confirmed His word with signs following, adding many thousands to His Kingdom. Each morning Paul Stern and I ministered to about a thousand emerging pastors and leaders in the great Swedish Philadelphia Church. John King, a dedicated young pastor in Bukavu, interpreted our messages in Swahili. Roger West and his team continue to invade the powers of darkness in that whole region with the compelling and unshakeable Gospel of The Kingdom of God.

(Paul Stern was called home to Heaven on February 19, 2013. Paul was truly a great general in the army of the Lord, my faithful brother in Christ, beloved husband to Eleanor, and dad to four dedicated children. He was blessed with a host of grandchildren and great grandkids, and they are all serving the Lord. Paul will be greatly missed. Well done, good and faithful servant of the Lord.)

My Treasure Chest

Many old gold mine areas are being re-screened. Abandoned mine shafts are being dug out again. The soaring price of gold compels men to re-visit old lodes of precious metals and search for residual gold. It is when the Word of the Lord is "precious," or scarce, that we start to dig again.

"That I may cause those who love me [wisdom] to inherit [true] riches and I will fill their treasuries" [130]

I want to provoke you to start digging again! The Lord says, "Call upon me and I will answer you and show you great and mighty things you have never known." [131]

Many years ago I met Dr. J. O. Kinnaman who had traveled with Sir Flinders Petrie, the renowned archeologist. As they drove along in their old Model T touring car Sir Petrie would suddenly stroke his beard and shout, "Stop!" He had spotted a "tell." He would order his servants to start digging

---

[130] In Proverbs 8:21 Amplified Bible
[131] Jeremiah 33:3

on the mound he sensed contained treasure. Frequently they unearthed amazing and valuable relics that had been buried for hundreds or even thousands of years. Among these findings was perhaps the greatest treasure ever unearthed: the Egyptian tomb of King Tutankhamun.

In my research for this memoire I have discovered many "serendipitous" treasures. They are to my spirit as many-faceted diamonds, brilliant gold nuggets, and hidden riches in secret places. The Lord God has ordained that He would "not do anything without first revealing His secret to his servants the prophets." [132] He also said,

"The secret things belong unto the Lord our God, but the things which are revealed belong to us and to our children forever, that we may do all the words of this law."[133]

```
If  we  don't  know,  then  we  need  a
teacher.
```

I treasure the many friendships with whom we have been wonderfully blessed. Some of them are well known people who have powerfully influenced the lives of multitudes. Others are more ordinary foot soldiers of the Cross who have done extraordinary things. Only in eternity will we discover how great so many unsung heroes are in God's sight.

In my youth I had set forth on this journey with a deeply-rooted sense of destiny. I cannot explain the many divinely appointed encounters that came my way in the early days. Providentially ordained relationships kept developing as the years went by. Much of what has transpired in my life can be traced back to my original discoveries in the Secret Place of the Most High. Precious nuggets of truth have been confirmed by prophecies and verified by an honest study of the Word. I have taken great pleasure over many years in seeing God watch over His word to perform it. I have also

---

[132] Amos 3:7

[133] Deuteronomy 29:29

discovered that the thing of which I am a part is greater than the part that I play. God's solution is always greater than my problem.

Rick Warren recently tweeted, "We are called human "beings," not human "doings." God is more interested in what I am that what I do. St. Catherine of Siena said, "Be what God meant you to be and you will set the World on fire." You are God's masterpiece *(Poema)* His poetry, custom made in His image.[134] All people have eternal existence (you will live forever somewhere) but not all people have eternal life. You see, you must be born again to have eternal life and to see His kingdom.[135] Jesus wants to live in you and in me. Jesus is our God who became man that we might become the sons of God by a new birth. God wrapped himself in Jesus. Jesus put a face on God. This glorious realization elevates you into a place of delightful expectation. We are linked with Omnipotence.

Beloved "Now" are we the sons of God, even though we may not know what we shall be, we know that when He appears we shall be like him! [136]

Augustine said, "Without God we cannot. Without us God will not." God has a history of taking seriously people who take His Word seriously. Throughout history God did not choose or use a man because he had arrived, but because he was willing to go somewhere with God. As E. M. Bounds would say, those God uses are "men on the stretch for God." I have discovered that God wants your life to be as beautiful as it was in the mind of God when he first thought of you.

It is so refreshing to know that God is getting you ready for that which is already ready for you.

Your eye hasn't seen it, your ear hasn't heard it, neither has it entered into your heart; the things that God has (already) prepared for them that love Him. But He has

---

[134] Ephesians 2:10
[135] John 3:3-5
[136] 1 John 3:1-3

revealed them to us through His Spirit. For the Spirit searches all things yes, the deep things of God...that we might know the things that have been freely given to us by God" [137]

If God has anything to do with you, He has everything to do with you. He is the author and the finisher of our faith. I want to assure you that the same Lord that has guided my little raft on this apostolic journey is absolutely faithful to His Word. From my earliest ventures to this present time I have found Him to be abundantly above all I could ask or think. The Lord has opened great doors of adventure into places that had been firmly closed. We watched the "latter rain" 1948 revival expand all over the earth. Healing meetings were abundant throughout our nations in the 1950s and '60s. We embraced the Jesus Movement that spread across several continents. It was our joy to partake in the charismatic renewal in the 1960s through the 1980s, seeing many believers from numerous denominations being filled with the Holy Spirit. But I believe the glory of the latter house shall be greater than the former. That means that the good old days are just ahead!

I hear the sound of abundance of rain. In spite of the totally confusing political scene, I believe I have heard a word from the Lord that He is clearing the stage to accomplish His eternal purposes. He has spoken to me about removing the tired old actors, many of whom have stopped playing by the Script(ures) and have tried to alter their message to appeal to a Biblically illiterate and spiritually distracted generation. One writer called it the "juvenilization" of the church. They are "dumbing down" the Gospel to appeal to the ignorant. Allow me to assure you that it was the plain, simple, unadulterated Gospel that gripped my young heart and persuaded me to forsake all else and follow Jesus.

I believe we are going to see a whole new cast, true to the Script, that will be led by a vanguard of youth who have been

---

[137] 1 Corinthians 2: 9-12

made willing as volunteers in the day of His power.[138] The Lord has promised to revive His work in the midst of the years, and to pour out His Spirit on all flesh. "Your sons and your daughters shall prophesy." Old men shall dream dreams, and the rest of us, young folks, are going to have our vision restored. For "where there is no prophetic vision, God's people cast off restraint. [139] Obscure truths are going to be rediscovered and preached with persuasive power. Karl Barth said: "He that walks the pathway of truth, treads the razor edge of heresy." God is confirming His Word with mighty signs and wonders. I am confident that I will live to see the Knowledge of His glory covering the earth as the waters cover the sea. [140]

There is a new generation poised to answer the call. I want to strongly state that it's the simple Gospel of Jesus that is the power of God unto salvation. I am thoroughly convinced that everything that this journey has accomplished must reflect to His glory. It is not by my ability, nor by my power, but by His Spirit that I have come this far by faith. I am eternally indebted to my Lord and to my family. They have been more precious to me than words can tell. My loving wife has truly been my "help meet" and loyal companion through many adventures over the past sixty years! My richest treasures are my wife and my family. It is primarily to them that I dedicate my *Chronicles*.

The Saga of Moses

I am frequently drawn to the amazing call and life of my namesake, Moses. I find that God doesn't waste anything. He uses all our experiences to prepare us. Moses' eighty years of training weren't wasted. His forty years in Pharaoh's palace prepared him to deal with Pharaoh. His forty years as a shepherd prepared him to lead God's people through the wilderness and into their destiny. God never wastes an

---

[138] Psalm 110:3
[139] Proverbs 29:18 NKJV
[140] Habakkuk 2:14

experience. Never! Somehow I feel I can relate to the "eighty years." Of course, the first Moses began his public ministry in his eightieth year. I wonder...

Set in the tapestry of the "Heroes of Faith" chapter is this rich nugget of truth about Moses.

"Prompted by faith Moses after his birth was concealed for three months by his parents...they saw that he was a proper child." [141]

God packed Moses' diaper bag, and it contained everything he need for his one hundred and twenty year journey. It was this awesome call of God that prompted Moses to forsake Egypt and fulfill his destiny as the second-greatest deliverer in human history. Israel knew the acts of God. Moses knew His ways.[142]

"Aroused by faith, Moses, when he had grown to maturity and become great, refused to be called the son of Pharaoh's daughter. Because he preferred to share the reproach of Christ, he could expect to receive from God greater riches than all the treasures of Egypt. He *"endured as seeing Him who was invisible."* He never flinched at the mandate that God had given him. Even when his own brother and sister challenged his leadership, his meekness shone forth. Moses trusted God to vindicate him with the budding of his rod. Supernatural signs and wonders verified God's choice and condemned his challengers.

The Exodus from Egypt was initiated by the blood of the Lamb being applied over the threshold of every Israeli dwelling. Every person inside that home, including their Egyptian neighbors, who believed God's word were covered and protected from the death angel. That night they partook of the roasted lamb, completing the Passover ritual. Everyone was miraculously healed as they bit into the lamb.[143] This was a precursor to the Table of the Lord where we "eat His flesh and drink His blood," and healing becomes

---

[141] Hebrews 11:23-29 Amplified Bible
[142] Psalm 103:7
[143] Psalm 105:37

the children's bread. There was not one feeble one among them (somewhere between three and six million Israelites), and everyone was miraculously endowed with silver and gold!

The Song of Moses

Great leaders, good and evil have emulated Moses' techniques that were given to Him by the Lord God Jehovah. The Lord gave Moses a song[144] that he sang to all of Israel. It was his swan song, and he was greater in the sunset of his life then at its zenith. The rabbis tell us that God "kissed his soul to death." The Lord Himself buried Moses in a secret place, and the Angel Michael disputed with the devil who was trying to claim Moses' body. Moses saw a city who's builder and maker is God. He forsook Egypt and *"endured steadfastly as one who gazed on Him who is invisible."*[145]

Thomas Carlyle wrote, "He who has no vision of eternity will never get a true grasp of time. Only God can give us back time. He restores the years that the ravaging locusts have devoured." [146]

It is this constant assurance of the call and vision that the Lord gave me in my teens and the fulfillment of His prophetic promises that have sustained me on my journey. I too found that my Lord heard my screams at birth on Hickory Road in Windsor in 1933. He packed my bags and provided abundantly above all that I could ask or think for my journey that was worthy of its destination. As for me and my house we have been blessed.

---

[144] Deuteronomy 32
[145] Hebrews 11:26-27
[146] Joel 2:25

The Vegh's fiftieth wedding anniversary with their dear family.

Birthday number eighty.
The happiest of them all.

Chapter Twenty   *The Trial of our Faith*

We thank the Lord for the many years of good health our family had enjoyed, but in April of 2006 Betty received quite a shock from her doctor. After a routine physical examination she was told that she had stage-three colon cancer. She was immediately scheduled for surgery and had the tumor removed. Betty was very strong during this trial and trusted the Lord completely for His will to be accomplished in her life. She had a miraculous recovery and new strength from the Lord to finish her task.

Our son Marcus, who was living in Coeur d'Alene, Idaho, at the time, came to visit his mom in the hospital in Irvine, California. Marcus prayed fervently for his mother to be healed, not knowing what the future held for us as a family. About three weeks later, Marcus was diagnosed with inoperable throat cancer, and he was given only three months to live. What a shock to us all! He had not been feeling well for some time, but his condition had not been correctly diagnosed. His doctor was treating him for acid reflux disease.

A Lasting Legacy

Fervent prayers were offered for Marcus' recovery, literally around the world. Marcus had ministered to so many people in multiple nations, gaining many friends in each field of labor.

He received many encouraging words at that time, and he fully trusted the Lord for His will to be done. Betty was so grateful that she was feeling strong enough to care for Marcus at our home. Later on the Lord graciously provided us with a beautiful new condominium in Coeur D'Alene (near the hospital). Our daughter Becky and her husband, Gail, spent many weeks there also, encouraging him daily.

Marcus, after his diagnosis, lived eighteen months, and was able to accomplish many projects. During this time the Lord was teaching us all the power of faith in God's Word.

Marcus had a remarkable recovery for a short season. During this time he had a powerful DVD interview at Saddleback Church with Kay Warren[147] that has been widely circulated.

Not "Why" Lord, but Who

These words were spoken by Marcus in that powerful interview. Marcus said, "I am not questioning 'why' this has happened to me, but 'who' it is that allowed it to happen." The Lord gave him a sure word from Isaiah.

> *"The righteous man perishes and no one lays it to heart; and merciful devout men are taken away, with no one considering that the uncompromisingly upright and godly person is taken away from the calamity and evil to come [even through wickedness]. He in death enters into peace; they rest in their beds, each one who walks straight and in his uprightness"*[148]

The Lord surely took him from the evil to come. Marcus is one of our "arrows" who has hit the mark in Heaven. Marcus, in his forty-seven years on earth, accomplished much. He was truly a visionary and a Kingdom man with a passion to make disciples for Jesus of all nations. He zealously pursued his life's calling and mission. Though he is dead, yet he speaks, especially among the hundreds of unreached, unlearned people groups that have no written language. Marcus continues to leave his mark and his passion for souls was as contagious as his ever-present, disarming smile. He had a God-given ability to impart that passion to everyone he talked to. He not only inspired others but showed and aided them through "progressive vision" to reach the unreached nations of the world.

---

[147] Mrs. Rick Warren
[148] Isaiah 57:1-2 The Amplified Bible

Marcus withRuth and Billy Graham

Marcus was a vital part of the "Table 71" group in Amsterdam at the Billy Graham World Conference on Evangelism. It was there that Marcus birthed the whole concept of "Finishing the Task" and his vision for "Following Jesus," which was the oral transcription of the whole Bible into story format. These outstanding Bible stories are now being translated into hundreds of languages around the world. Marcus had teamed with some of the world's leading missionaries, and he left an indelible mark on so many like Hector Tamez and Paul Eshleman who are now carrying on his vision of "Finishing the Task."

The *Finishing The Task* initiative which Marcus began is now called the *Issachar Initiative.* It now involves over one thousand mission organizations and churches, who have sent out 9,544 full-time missionaries into 870 unengaged, unreached people groups, and planted over 20,000 churches."

Hector recently told us that the Lord gave him access to over 120,000 people with the materials that Marcus had provided in "Finishing the Task." Hector has also trained hundreds of young ministers who are faithfully following Jesus to the most remote areas of Mexico and Central and

South America. Marcus' words and materials continue to be an inspiration to the newly formed "Sons of Issachar." You can hear his passionate plea for prayer for the Lord of the Harvest to thrust forth laborers. (Visit "Finishing the Task" on the web-site.[149]) These "Sons of Issachar" are leaders joining ranks with dedicated "disciplers" all over the world to reach every corner of this world with the Gospel by 2025.

Marcus didn't just talk about ministry. He lived it, and he showed others how to do it. He was so innovative in his technical skills and he was directly involved in transforming the Jesus Film into a DVD format, which has now been distributed to over forty million people in hundreds of languages. He was a team player and he was most assuredly on God's team. Marcus was sold out for Jesus and was consumed with finishing his task. He had traveled extensively to over fifty-four countries and he lived his life to the fullest for his Savior and his family. He was a glorious example of what God can and will do with a life that is totally sold out to Him. His life is a living epistle that is known and read by all, and we can learn so much from it.

When Marcus was about four years old we entertained a missionary from China. Brother Hsao said in his message that every fourth child born in this world is Chinese. Marcus, our fourth-born, looked up at his Mom and said, "Mom, am I Chinese?" He wasn't Chinese, but He went on to be a mighty force for God in China. His "Finishing the Task" material is now distributed to hundreds of thousands of Chinese believers. The seeds of greatness were

Marcus with Annelisa, Matthew, and Hunter

---

and still are sprouting! Marcus even as a young child, was our weeping "Jeremiah" who often travailed in prayer around the church altars. He spent much time teaching his three young children, Annelisa, Matthew, and Hunter the great Bible stories and the value and power of prayer.

During his last days in the Hospital in Coeur D'Alene, our whole family, his siblings, and his three children walked with Marcus to the edge of eternity. We spent precious days praying, singing, worshipping, and listening to Marcus tell of his great desire to be in heaven, to meet his precious Lord and Savior whom he had served so faithfully. Marcus had shown us how to live, and then he showed us how to die peacefully and enter into the presence of the Lord. He passed on to glory with a smile on his face and a song on his lips the morning of October 20, 2007.

Our first memorial service for Marcus was in Post Falls, Idaho, at his home church, Real Life Ministries, where he had served as an elder. His brother-in-law Gail Sterling officiated. We then had a second memorial service in Saddleback Church with Pastor Rick Warren officiating. Many of Marcus' colleagues in missions, and several pastor friends, also shared in the service. Marcus and his family had been members of Saddleback church for several years previously, and he had a close fellowship with Pastor Rick Warren. Marcus had his service pre-planned. We knew who he wanted to minister at his memorial service. Marcus loved his friends, and from his very early days he was a God anointed inspiration to all who knew him.

We have grateful hearts as we render this tribute to Marcus our son and are so very thankful for the Lord giving him to us for forty-seven short years. Marcus was a wonderful son to Betty and I, a faithful father, and a dear brother; not only to his own siblings but to all the body of Christ.

One day Heaven's books will be opened and we shall all stand before the judgment seat of Christ, we shall then give account for all that we did and did not do![150] "So we make it our goal to please Him." May we all determine to be faithful to our Lord Jesus so that one day we can all hear Him say, "Well done good and faithful servants, enter into the joy of your Lord."

Betty and I look forward to finishing our task and finishing strong, with our "arrows" in hand. We will stand before our blessed Lord and Savior, with grateful hearts for all His faithfulness in all our lives and in our years of active ministry. It will be worth it all when we see Jesus.

We shall be united with our loved ones, and with our beloved son, Marcus, who are now in the grandstands of Glory. These folks are called "a great cloud of witnesses," and they are among the real "Who's-Who" you find in Hebrews eleven. Then we will meet with many of you who have so blessed and influenced our lives in so many countries. We are living in anticipation of a grand reunion, above all with Jesus our Lord.

Betty and Moses Vegh with Marcus' children, September, 2012

Today in vision I am standing on my Mt. Nebo[151] as Moses did. In my eightieth year I am looking forward and outward, not backward. Moses' unabated vision scanned the great legacy of Israel. I also see a mighty unshakeable Kingdom on the horizon, coming with a great harvest of nations being gathered in from the four corners of the earth. With the Lord's help we will finish strong! My little

---

[150] II Corinthians 5: 9-11
[151] Deuteronomy 33:4

189

raft is still being borne along by the winds of inspiration, just a little slower now.

I have sensed something akin to standing with Moses on that mountain recently, when the Lord reminded me not to be like the old guy who never stirred the sugar in his tea so he could get it all in the last gulp. Betty and I have been stirring the sugar in our cups, and it gets sweeter every day. We want to finish the task that the Lord has given us and keep it sweet.

I am thrilled by the prospect of seeing millions of young people turning to the Lord in these last days, uninhibited by religion or tradition, totally sold out to a mighty Savior. Upon your sons and daughters the Lord will pour out of His Spirit and they shall prophesy![152] Our Grandson Caleb and many more of our children and grandchildren will be in that number. This fearless remnant will know their God indeed and do mighty exploits.[153] They will "finish the task" with the same exuberant joy in the Holy Spirit that Marcus had, which was also the hallmark of the young church in action portrayed in the book of Acts. There will be a great army of youth who will be anointed by the Spirit, ready and willing in the day of His power.[154] They shall offer themselves willingly as volunteers. Jesus will build His Church, and His unshakeable Kingdom shall come!

Our eyes have seen the glory of the coming of our Lord, and we have been ignited with a holy fervor and great expectation. I hear again the sound of abundance of rain! The harbingers of the end times cause us to lift up our heads and rejoice, for our King is coming. We are admonished to have ample oil in our lamps to go out and meet Him.[155] We are looking to our great God and Savior to call us home.

It has been exciting partnering with Jesus on the Acts of an Apostolic Journey. We have remembered our call to be

---

[152] Joel 2: 28
[153] Daniel 11:32
[154] Psalm 110:3
[155] Mathew 25:6

190

"ambassadors of hope" to the nations, and we will continue on our journey, since I can't find the word "retire" in the Bible. Betty and I will confidently ride along on our little raft and trust our great Captain to guide us safely to our desired haven.

This is our legacy for you our family, our extended family, and our many friends and readers. May the God of grace be with you, as you commit your life wholly to the Lord. We pray the Aaronic blessing upon you.

"The Lord bless you and keep you; The Lord make His face to shine upon you, and be gracious unto you; The Lord lift up His countenance upon you and give you peace," the shalom of God.[156]

---

[156] Numbers 6: 23-27

Made in the USA
San Bernardino, CA
15 October 2013